BATTERED WOMEN

SAGE FOCUS EDITIONS

BATTERED WOMEN

EDITOR

DONNA M. MOORE

SAGE PUBLICATIONS   Beverly Hills/London

For information address:

SAGE PUBLICATIONS, INC.
275 South Beverly Drive
Beverly Hills, California 90212

SAGE PUBLICATIONS LTD
28 Banner Street
London ECIY 8QE England

Printed in the United States of America

Library of Congress Cataloging in Publication Data

Main entry under title:

Battered women.

   (Sage focus editions ; 9)
   Bibliography: p.
   1. Wife abuse—United States—Addresses, essays, lectures. I. Moore, Donna M. II. Series.
HV6626.B34   364.1'55   79-982
ISBN 0-8039-1162-9
ISBN 0-8039-1163-7 pbk.

FIRST PRINTING

CONTENTS

EDITOR'S INTRODUCTION
An Overview of the Problem

Donna M. Moore

Violence by men against women, and specifically against their wives or living partners, is not a new problem; it is assumed by some to have begun with the first monogamous pairing. What *is* new, however, is public admission that wife beating occurs in "civilized" countries and the insistence by women and men in those countries that such violence is no longer acceptable and that we must begin discussing the problem and searching for solutions which will put an end to such violence. The open discussion, exploration of causes, and search for solutions is what this book is about. Our hope is that the reader will become deeply engrossed in the problem as (s)he reads the book—that we will involve you in both the discussion and in the quest for solutions.

What is the Problem?

Battering Defined

Violence has become so widespread in American society, and because so many people are currently writing and talking about both its source and its solution, it is important to understand more precisely how the authors represented in this book define battering. There are two ways in which a woman might be abused: physically and psychologically. The majority of the material in this book relates specifically to physical abuse defined as "deliberate, severe, and repeated physical injury . . . with the minimal injury being severe bruising."[1] We also recognize the psychological damage which one person can do to another by using fear, guilt, or psychological abuse of a life-threatening nature. We will, therefore, use the terms *abused, battered,* and *beaten* interchangeably to indicate either severe physical or psychological damage.

Although we recognize that there is increasing data and concern about both men as the victims of battering and about child abuse as part of the overall picture of violence in the family,[2] we are addressing ourselves in this book only to women as the battered and men as the batterers. This focus is intended to imply only that this is our particular area of expertise, and we look to others to heighten our awareness regarding men and children as victims.

And finally, because we recognize that women who are being abused may not be married to their batterer, we will use the terms *battered women, battered wives, battered spouses,* and *battered partners* interchangeably. Thus we are discussing physical violence against women by the men with whom they are married or cohabiting.

History of Battering

English common law, upon which most of America's laws are patterned, gave husbands the right to chastise their wives. Sue Eisenberg and Patti Micklow point out that the "rule of thumb" refers to the right of a husband to beat his wife with a stick "no thicker than his thumb."[3] In 1824 the Supreme Court of Mississippi acknowledged the husband's right to beat his wife. Similar decisions were rendered in both Maryland

and Massachusetts. In 1974 North Carolina modified this position by stating:

> the husband has no right to chastise his wife, under any cir-
> cumstances . . . [however] if no permanent injury has been
> inflicted, nor malice, cruelty, nor dangerous violence shown
> by the husband, it is better to draw the curtain, shut out the
> public gaze, and leave the parties to forget and forgive.[4]

Unfortunately, the court did not define permanent injury, malice, cruelty, or dangerous violence which effectively implemented an attitude of noninterference with family or domestic disputes which still exists in large measure today.

Toward the end of the nineteenth century, courts began changing their decisions and no longer supported, across the board, the husband's right to chastise his wife. As early as 1871 a Massachusetts court openly denied that wife beating was acknowledged by law.

The courts have been in considerable disagreement over the years regarding not only the issue of a man's right to beat his wife but also on the questions of what a woman's recourse was and whether interspousal immunity from assault charges should be observed.[5] It does appear, however, that with recent pressure from both within and without the legal profession, the courts are beginning to consider wife beating unacceptable, to give women access to legal remedies, and to take serious steps in sentencing batterers. It has been too long coming; for many women who have been beaten beyond physical or psychological repair or who have been literally beaten to death, it has come too late. But it is happening and like other legal changes it is intricately interwoven with social and cultural attitudes. Chapter 3 by Eva Jefferson Paterson and Chapter 4 by Sandra Blair both discuss relationships between legal and social attitudes and ways in which we might continue effecting changes.

Causes for Battering and Current Concerns

One might ask both why battering occurs and why something that has been happening for centuries should be a matter of so much current concern. Close examination of the literature about battering leads me to believe that there are three major clusters of reasons which account for the occurrence of battering.

The first cluster is *societal* and begins with the definition of families as being both nonviolent and inviolate. Traditionally, the home is where people retreat for safety, love, and solace. For a society to recognize and admit that this is not true of the American home would be to admit that the family unit may be in trouble; further, to admit that the family unit is in trouble would require that each of us take a close look at our own family and recognize that this could happen to us, too. It is much easier and safer, both socially and personally, to continue the myth of the nonviolent family. Thus, society either approves of battering as acceptable behavior or ignores it and does not provide the social help network which is effective in aiding battered women and their children in leaving a violent home. In Chapter 1, Del Martin explores societal reasons for both the occurrence and the continuance of battering.

A second set of reasons which allow battering to occur and go unrecognized and unresolved is *legal*. Our legal system consists of legislators, police officers, district attorneys, and judges. Police hesitate to get involved because it is both dangerous and difficult to deal with domestic disputes.[6] Further, as Sandra Blair points out in Chapter 4, there are no rewards for police officers in working on domestic violence cases. If the police do not make a good arrest and perform a good investigation, the district attorney cannot take a case to court. The district attorney also does not get many rewards for successfully prosecuting a batterer. And the judge cannot find a person guilty and/or sentence appropriately if the law does not allow him/her to do so. The entire legal system from civil and criminal laws to programmatic legislation to police officers, district attorneys, and judges is intricately interwoven. None of these components operates independently of the others, and the laws as currently written and implemented simply do not work effectively for battered women.

Personal and/or psychological factors become the third major set of reasons battering occurs. In both Chapter 1 by Del Martin and Chapter 2 by Lenore Walker we find discussion of how people's attitudes about acceptable male and female behaviors lead to a psychological expectation and acceptance of physical violence by men against women. When we behave in a sex-role stereotyped manner toward children and expect them to act as "little boys and little girls," we are rewarding male children for becoming independent, aggressive, controlling, and unemotional. Conversely, we are rewarding female children for becoming dependent, passive, noncontrolling, and emotional. These are the very behaviors that males and females carry into adulthood and marriage which leads to the acceptability of the man's taking charge of a relationship and the woman's accepting his control, even if that control assumes a violent form. Additionally, we must recognize that as long as we see battering as something abnormal which happens only to sick people, we protect ourselves psychologically from thinking that it might happen to us, and thus we negate the need for solutions.

Why, then, are we looking at these issues today if we have so many reasons for not doing so?

First, society is beginning to take a serious look at the issues of violence in all areas of our lives. Part of the concern about violence has taken us into the home to look at abused children. Once we have entered the homes of abused children we see and cannot dismiss the fact that the women in many of those homes are also being brutalized.

Second, the legal profession and law enforcement agencies in particular have begun to take seriously their role as social change agents. Many police officers, district attorneys, and judges are beginning to see themselves as helping agents for society rather than as simple implementers of the law.

Third, the feminist movement has begun to force a new definition of what is an acceptable amount and use of force or violence against women. Further, women are beginning to use their own battering as a major defense in cases in which they have committed homicide against their batterer. There have been over a dozen cases of this type in the past few years which have received widespread publicity and which have served to put men and the legal profession on notice that women are refusing to accept being battered any longer. The more famous either the victim or the batterer in such a homicide case, the more publicity it is likely to receive and the more likely it is to affect our notions about battering and self-defense. As such cases become more frequent and receive public attention, it becomes impossible to ignore issues of battering and their effects on family and society.

Whatever the reasons, public recognition of battering is here and brings with it a need to be more specific about how often it happens, who does it, why they do it, how women respond to it, and how we might end it.

How Often Does It Happen?

Wife battering is assumed by many people to be the most underreported crime in America.[7] It is difficult to obtain accurate and meaningful data regarding its frequency because social agencies, law enforcement agencies, and private individuals (physicians, attorneys, counselors) who most frequently come into contact with battered women either do not recognize the battering, have no need or means by which to report such incidents, or would prefer not to get involved because of the attitude that it is a private affair.[8]

Because battering occurs almost exclusively within the privacy of the home[9] where there are often no witnesses, and because those who do observe or overhear such violence prefer not to become involved, data are rarely available. Further, those who do observe family violence or suspect that it is happening tend to shy away from those families and not put themselves in the position of any further witnessing behavior.

Because of the image of the family as nonviolent, a two-way isolation occurs: possible witnesses disengage themselves from battered friends and victims and/or batterers avoid friends and others in order not to reveal themselves to further observations. Thus, not only have we removed possible witnesses and sources of support for these women but we have also removed possible data-gathering sources.

Seriously gathering data and learning about wife abuse means learning about a depressing and frightening phenomenon. Although the data are haphazard, there are some statistics relating to specific areas of the country and some national data regarding the status of the problem. I offer a few selected examples as an indication of the scope of battering:

Kansas City, Missouri, 1976. The Police Department revealed that 90% of the city's family homicides had been preceded by at least one call to the Police Department, and in 50% of those cases the police had been called five or more times.

Washtenaw County, Michigan. Thirty-five percent of all assault cases are wife assault.

Dade County, Florida. Over a nine-month period, 1,000 cases of battered women were handled.

Montgomery County, Maryland. The Wife Assault Task Force handled 650 incidents during its first year of operation.

Michigan. One county reported 42.4% of all assault complaints in a five-month period were wife assault.

Brooklyn Legal Services, 1976. Fifty-seven percent of the women filing for divorce complained of physical assaults for approximately four years before seeking divorce.

Cleveland, Ohio, 1971. Thirty-seven percent of females filing for divorce complained of physical abuse when filing.

Marvin E. Wolfgang studied 588 cases of criminal homicide in 1958 and concluded that 87% of all female victims were slain by males and 84% of female offenders slew males. The predominant reasons for such murders were sex, love, and family matters. Wolfgang stated that slayings with excessive degrees of violence predominate in the home and are most likely to involve a spousal relationship in which the wife is the victim of the husband's brutal beating.[10]

Donald T. Lunde reported in *Psychology Today* in 1975 that approximately 40% of homicides in the United States are spouses killing spouses.[11]

Nationwide estimates predict that up to 60% of American families will experience interspousal violence during the course of a relationship.

The latest study by Straus et al. found violence in 28% of all American families. Lenore Walker estimates that violence occurs between 50% of all American marital partners.[12]

Nationwide, the FBI estimates that wife abuse occurs three times as frequently as sexual assault, and they further estimate that it is reported less than 10% of the time. This would mean that wife abuse occurs approximately every 18 seconds somewhere in the United States.

Sabra Wooley[13] reminds us that statistics are easy to manipulate, criticize, or ignore. What cannot be easily dismissed, however, is the testimony of those women who have experienced battering and those who are working directly with the problem such as police officers, district attorneys, social workers, physicians, and shelter workers. In an attempt to substantiate battering statistics, she points out that when a shelter becomes available it is immediately overwhelmed with residents This phenomenon is nationwide, in both rural and urban locations. Del Martin reinforces this finding by saying that shelters are always filled to capacity and have waiting lists before they actually open their doors.

Clearly, we must develop better tools to define the extent of the problem. In the meantime, however, battered women and those working with them speak loud and clear: the problem is a human one, not a statistical one, and it is time for us to sit up and take notice of the violence occurring against women within the American family.

The Batterer

Who Is This Man?

While it would be easy to portray the wife beater as a monster who is psychologically deranged, several major researchers[14] point out that this is simply not true. Langley and Levy[15] cite Sue Steinmetz who labels this the "psychopathology myth." She argues that most batterers are not psychotics, psychopaths, or the demented few. They are ordinary men who have low levels of self-esteem, who have learned male role behavior from their parents, and who continue to play out the violent part of that role when life stresses become intolerable. While some continue to believe that batterers are "sick," most people today would agree that we are dealing with an average man who is under some unusual stress and/or who has learned his masculine role, especially as it relates to socially acceptable aggression, only too well. Langley and Levy further point out that to try to classify batterers into types might be useful, but it also tends to set them aside as different from us, thus allowing the rest of the population to breathe a sigh of relief that it could not happen to them.

Batterers represent all ages, all educational levels, all religions, all socioeconomic classes, and all regions of the country and city.[16] It has also been well substantiated by Langley and Levy that while official police and hospital records show a higher assault rate among the poor, the unofficial records of shelters, hot lines, private physicians, attorneys, and other helping professionals show no such class differences. The major reason for the difference in public records may be that the wealthy have greater resources; wealthy women who are battered can go to a private physician, a private counselor, a private attorney, or leave home with their own financial resources, while poorer women must use public agencies and thus end up as part of the statistical pool.

In summary, what batterers do appear to have in common is a low level of self-esteem, a learned response of violence to stress, and very traditional concepts of acceptable masculine and feminine behavior.

Why Does He Do It?

Summarizing the information available, I will look at the three major contributors to wife beating: frustration/stress, sex roles or learned behavior, and alcohol.

There seems to be general agreement that frustration or stress in a man's life is one of the major reasons he will beat his spouse.[17] Most often these frustrations have little to do with the woman involved but may be related to work, money, interpersonal relationships outside of the home, or parenting pressures. The woman simply becomes the target of his violent explosion. Frustration may be a result of differences between the man's expectations of himself and the reality of his life. Thus, if he has high expectations but is not successful (in his own image of himself), this may lead to frustration. If he indeed accepts the cultural image of men as being strong, in control, and unemotional, he may be unable to talk about his frustration with anyone. These stresses may then lead to a violent eruption with his wife as the target. Other data suggest that these men may be insecure, moody, and dependent on their wives in addition to being hostile and aggressive. They are also reported to be severely jealous of their wives.[18] Lisa Leghorn[19] reminds us, however, that women also have frustrations but they do not usually beat their husbands or otherwise act out in physical ways. Further, in looking for answers, we need to look at the many men who experience frustration but do not resort to physical violence as a solution to their problems.

A second major cause for men beating their wives is that of sex-role socialization and learned behavior. The American culture provides stereotyped notions of what is masculine and what is feminine. Men are aggressive, in control of both themselves and others, heads of their households, and un-emotional. Irene Frieze points out that power differentials in the wife's favor (such as she is more educated, makes more money, is more influential in the community) might challenge the man's masculine prerogatives thus producing frustration which leads to stress and battering. When either the male or the female in a home has extremely traditional views of the male and female roles, frustration or stress based on these roles is likely to lead to battering.[20] For example. if a man feels it is his masculine prerogative to be in control of both himself and his wife, and if his wife has more community status, more education, or earns more money, he may feel he is not a man. On the other hand, if this same woman has learned to believe that the man in a family should indeed have more status, more education, and more power, she may feel that she is not being very feminine. One way to make herself more feminine, and to let her husband be more masculine, is to let him regain control through physical or psychological abuse. This scenario seems to be effective when either, or both, partner has a tra-ditional view of appropriate sex-role behaviors and when the current reality does not fall within that traditional picture, thus necessitating some means of return to tradition. Often that return occurs through male abuse of the female to regain his masculine control and to let her play out her feminine dependency. Further, when a man is unable to meet his own expectations of the masculine sex role, low self-esteem results and he sometimes attempts to raise his self-concept by beating his wife.

Another behavior men learn as children is how to handle anger and aggression. If the man comes from a home in which either his mother has been battered or he has been abused as a child, his earlier training and experience has taught him that physical violence is an acceptable response to anger. In other words, when children observe their mothers being battered, they grow up assuming that this is the way men and women resolve their differences. Also, men who have been beaten as children have learned that the one who loves them has the right, and often the responsibility (for example, "I wouldn't do this if I didn't love you"), to beat them. If the man has learned and adopted the traditional stereotypic masculine role behavior, and if he has come from a family in which violence occurred and was accepted, he is more likely to be a batterer than if these conditions had not existed for him.[21] Families are basic training grounds for both sex roles and for acceptability of violence.

Irene Frieze summarizes this by saying that she feels battering occurs when there is some form of stress in a man's life coupled with violence as a learned response to frustration such that stress automatically elicits violence because the person knows no other form of response.

Alcohol is the third reason often given for why a man beats his wife. While the rate of alcohol use during battering incidents is often as high as 60%,[22] there is a great deal of debate regarding cause and effect. Richard Gelles points out that violence does occur without alcohol being present, and alcohol is often consumed without violence resulting. Women also use alcohol heavily without committing violence against a spouse. What, then, is the relationship? Most researchers[23] currently agree that alcohol in battering homes is used to give both the batterer and the battered an excuse for the beating. Women use a man's alcohol consumption as a way of explaining his behavior: "He only did it because he was drunk." Men also use it as an excuse: "I didn't know what I was doing—if only I could control my drinking." In other words, alcohol excuses what otherwise would be unacceptable behavior. It not only relieves the man of responsibility for his behavior but it also gives the wife justification for remaining in the situation in the hope that he will quit drinking and then quit beating. While reducing alcohol abuse might reduce battering somewhat, no one seems to argue that it would stop battering altogether.

It seems important to point out that one of the major reasons we know so little about batterers is that most of them will not recognize or admit that their behavior is unacceptable; therefore they will not seek outside help. Our largest source of information about batterers comes from the women whom they batter. Women seek and accept assistance, and in the process they tell us what they can about the men who beat them. Clearly, we need to begin devising means of obtaining information directly from batterers if we are to both understand and change their behavior.

What Makes Him Stop?

Most women who have lived with battering men agree that there is no way to predict when a man is going to beat her.[24] The lack of predictability lends, of course, to the fear and stress a woman experiences—always needing to be prepared for potential abuse.

Unfortunately, since we know so little about what makes a man beat his spouse, information about what makes him stop beating her is even more scarce. If we look at the data about why he does it—frustration, learned violent behavior, sex-role expectations, low self-esteem, and alcohol—we might assume that changing any of those conditions would also stop the beating. That is, if we can teach him to use behaviors other than violence when responding to frustration or stress, if we help him understand that traditional sex roles are not the only way (or even the most effective way) to relate to a woman and to one's self as a man, if we can help him elevate his self-esteem, and if we teach him to control his alcohol use, then we might see a decrease in the amount of battering that occurs. The most effective way to get men to seek and accept therapy is for the woman to either leave him or threaten to leave him if he does not seek help to change his battering behavior. This means, of course, that we must have therapy available for men who finally admit that they need help and wish to change abusive behaviors. Therapy for male batterers is becoming available throughout the country, with many programs reporting high success rates through the use of either behavior modification or group therapy. Clearly, this is one of the most unmapped areas of exploration in the whole arena of spouse abuse. We must learn how to work with male batterers and make therapy more accessible for such men so that we can stop battering altogether, not just decrease or control its frequency and severity.

The Battered Woman

Who Is She?

The profile of the battered woman looks almost identical to that of her batterer: she is all ages, all ethnicities, from all socioeconomic groups, has a low level of self-esteem, and for the most part has very traditional notions of male and female behavior. She may feel that her husband is supposed to be in charge of the family, even if that means beating her; she must be supportive of him, even if that means allowing herself to be abused repeatedly. Her role as a woman includes marriage, even a bad marriage, and to leave the home would be to admit that she is a failure as a woman.

Why Does She Stay?

There are many reasons why a woman continues to live in a home where she is being abused; indeed the complexity of reasons almost defies answering the question. The major reasons, which I will summarize here, include dependency, fear, social stigma, home and love, and psychological pressures.[25]

One of the most compelling reasons for a woman remaining in a battering home is that of dependency: physical, financial, and emotional. Battered women who are not working outside of the home, or who are extremely traditional in their sex-role behaviors, are particularly vulnerable to such dependency. If the man is her only form of financial support, it is ludicrous to suggest that she leave him. How else can she survive? Unless we can offer her the support she needs to either receive job training or obtain a job and reestablish her life, we may just as well continue to ignore her. In Chapter 1 Del Martin examines the difficulties women face in leaving home and obtaining financial, legal, and social assistance from public agencies. Not only do most forms of public assistance require a considerable amount of time to obtain after application for such help, but in most states a woman must have already applied for separation or divorce before she is eligible for such aid. The time lag and the necessity for legal action to terminate a marriage is often enough to discourage a woman from leaving her home. Without financial assistance, housing, or job training, the feeling of dependency upon one's husband is a reality many women cannot overcome. If the woman is extremely traditional in her views of men, women, and marriage, and if her self-esteem is indeed low, the red tape involved in ending a marriage and struggling to get public assistance is often the final blow to any desire she may have of leaving home.

Additionally, the data regarding women's financial dependence on men is overwhelming in both volume and impact. Even if women are working, or can be trained to obtain jobs, they will continue to make lower salaries than men in all fields and particularly if they have never worked. Many women must depend on the promise of either alimony or child support to get them through the financial strain of beginning new lives. However, fewer than 50% of divorced women in this country are awarded alimony by the courts. Child support presents an even larger problem. A ten-year study of child support ordered by the court showed that only 38% of husbands fully complied with the court order the first year following the divorce; 42% did not make any payment at all during the first year. The older the judgment was, the fewer the men who paid child support. During the tenth year after divorce, only 13% of the men were paying full child support, while 79% were paying nothing at all.[26] Thus it is important to understand when working with battered women that promises of alimony or child support are not very realistic answers to financial needs.

A second major reason for a woman staying in an abusive home is fear—fear of death if she stays, and fear of the unknown if she leaves.[27] Although she knows only too well that her current battering is endangering her life, and perhaps the lives of her children, she also is afraid to leave and experience the loneliness, financial devastation, failure, possible loss of friends and family, and fear of the unknown. It is a very drastic and lonely move for her to consider. After all, if the one who loves you treats you like that, what might the rest of the world do to you?[28] Another fear she has is that her husband will follow her if she leaves home to hunt her down and beat her again. These fears are not unfounded. Up to 50% of these husbands have sought out and continued to beat or terrorize their wives.[29] This is why shelters find it essential to protect access to and public knowledge of their locations. If the battered wife decides to stay in the home and report her beatings to police departments or other agencies, she must also fear the visit by a police officer and/or the arrest which may result which often makes the man so angry that his beatings increase—a risk she is often not willing to take. Police officers are also often unwilling to let the woman take that risk and will sometimes discourage arrest of her partner.[30] Further, if her husband is arrested he may lose time at work, lose his job altogether, or at least have to expend valuable financial resources on bail. These losses also affect her security and become a consideration in her decision regarding whether or not to call the police or otherwise report her beatings.

Social stigma is often a factor in a woman's decision about whether to leave. In Chapter 2 Lenore Walker talks about social stigma, so I will merely cite three types of situations which affect a decision to leave an abusive home. They include embarrassment to admit that her marriage has been bad, embarrassment or guilt that either she or others will feel that the beatings were deserved and that she was responsible for her own victimization, and embarrassment that she has stayed in such a bad situation for so long. Each of these factors may lead to a woman's decision to remain in the home rather than admit to having been the victim of an abusive home.

A very important reason why a battered wife chooses to stay with her husband is a combination of hope and love. This is often overlooked by advocates of battered women. It is important to remember that there are very strong bonds between these two people, just as there are with any cohabiting or marital partners.[31] She may stay because she loves this man when he is not beating her and holds out the hope that each beating will be the last.[32] A woman faces a real conflict with regard to this hope. If she leaves the home temporarily in order that she and her husband can change their responses to each other and then reunite, she may fear that such changes will decrease the likelihood that he wants her back. If she does not leave, there is very little chance that either of them will change their violent responses to each other.[33] In Chapter 2 Lenore Walker discusses the need for the couple to be separated while such changes are being developed if they are to change at all. It is also important to recognize how the cycles Dr. Walker discusses lend to the woman's continual hope that her mate will change, since he tells her after each beating how sorry he is and how he intends to change. This is a very romantic time which feeds right into her traditional background and the notion that love can conquer all. Tied to this hope is a sense of loyalty to a person whom she loves. How can she leave him now when he is so intent on changing?[34] In talking with 100 battered women in England, J. J. Gayford[35] asked women how they felt about their batterers: 36% just wanted the man out of their lives; 31% were indifferent; 11% felt pity for the man, and 21% felt affection or love for him. It is this 21% which would hang on indefinitely in the hope that each beating will be the last and they can then have the ideal relationship which her traditional and romantic notions of marriage have led her to expect.

And finally, there are a whole series of psychological reasons behind a woman's staying in an abusive home: shock that the person who says he loves her can treat her this way; guilt that she may indeed be responsible for his anger or her own beating; depression that she finds herself in a relationship which seems so hopeless and within which she feels so helpless (keep in mind also that depression is most often considered an internalized form of anger which women are especially afraid to express if they are traditionally feminine); humiliation that anyone would consider her so bad that they have to beat her; and an overall resulting low level of self-esteem which serves to keep her immobilized both physically and psychologically.

A result of this psychological impact is an intense isolation. The woman often avoids friends for fear they will ask questions about her injuries or discuss topics about relationships which she feels might come too close for her psychological comfort. If she does discuss the situation with friends or family they very often either do not believe her or avoid her thereafter out of their own fears or their feeling that they cannot help her. The net result is either a self-imposed or other-imposed isolation, but the result is the same; she has no resources upon which to draw information, support, or self-esteem.[36] Further, if she does share her problem with a friend but continues to remain within the relationship, the friend (no matter how concerned) will eventually become frustrated that the woman will not leave and will discontinue supporting or listening to her.

In an attempt to uncover what battered women feel causes their battering, Irene Frieze[37] found that when women attribute their beatings to themselves, guilt and self blame occur; if they had come from abusive homes as children, they might attribute the beatings to the marital state in general; if they attributed the beatings to a characteristic of their husbands, they were most likely to look for a way to leave the relationship.

Why Does She Leave?

Given all the reasons women choose to stay in an abusive home, one might well ask a different question: What gives some women the strength to leave?

Irene Frieze[38] outlines a series of events which seem to give women the strength they need to leave. As stated above, they are more likely to leave if they attribute the beatings to some characteristic of their husband than if they feel it is their own fault. They are also more likely to leave if they feel the beatings are going to continue than if they feel they are due to some temporary stress on their husbands which will decrease soon. In other words, they finally give up all hope for change.

Richard Gelles[39] has argued that the best predictor of a woman making a decision to leave is her independence, which is measured by whether or not she has a job. Women who work are more likely to leave home than women who do not. First, of course, the working woman has the financial means of caring for herself. Second, as a woman works outside the home she is also able to become aware of other, less violent lifestyles available to her and thus begins to reevaluate the seriousness of her own situation.[40]

A woman is far more likely to leave if she has a system of support for leaving. This support can come from friends, family, women's groups, shelters, churches, or any other person(s) who let her know that she is really okay and need not take such abuse. Unfortunately, however, most battered women who do seek out support for leaving find people giving them ideas about how to make the relationship better, which once again puts the responsibility for changing the situation back on her shoulders.

Further, a woman is more likely to leave a battering home if she does not have children, for a number of reasons. She may be able to find a home for herself but finding one which will accept children is much harder. Children require both additional financial resources and additional emotional energy. The children may love their father, and she may be reluctant to separate the family. And, of course, the husband often uses the children to increase her guilt and necessitate maintaining the family unit. On the other hand, a woman with children may stay only as long as she is the only one being beaten; for many women it is when the children start being beaten that she finally gathers the strength to leave her spouse.

And finally, a woman is more likely to leave as the battering gets more violent and frequent. Very few women leave a man after he hits her the first time.

Solutions

It is easy, given the intricate nature of this problem, for the abused woman to feel overwhelmed and desperate. However, there are solutions. Conversely, we must recognize that this issue has been accepted and covered up for centuries. We cannot anticipate, in view of past history, that we can solve the problem overnight. We must continue utilizing temporary relief for individual women while also working on the development of long-term solutions. The solutions will be slow; slower than most of us want them to be, and too late for some women who will be literally beaten to death while we formulate solutions. It seems imperative, then, that everyone work together to seek creative solutions before today's children grow up to be tomorrow's batterers and battered. Since I have classified the major causes of battering as being social, legal, and psychological/personal, I will also look at solutions in those terms.

Social Solutions

Perhaps the foremost social solution to battering is to educate people regarding the issue and attempt to change both public attitudes and behaviors toward battering. We must obtain new legislation, insist that legal agencies enforce the laws, obtain funding for needed social services, and find the answers to many very knotty problems.

We need immediate assistance for women who are being physically abused by their spouses. We need housing so women can have shelter for themselves and their children while they begin rebuilding their lives; we need emergency financial assistance funds—money we can give women immediately in the middle of the night or on the weekends without going through days or weeks of paperwork with social service or welfare agencies; we need hot lines women can call and get emotional support and information about where the physical and financial resources are.

We need counseling services for both women and men. These must not be services that will help women adjust to their unhealthy homes but services which help both the man and the woman stop the battering.

We need crisis management programs within social service agencies and law enforcement agencies which go beyond temporary separation and immediate counseling of victims.[41] We need crisis management which is aimed at changing the situation rather than simply calming it down so it will be temporarily safer (but not really safe) for the family.

We need the type of feminist advocacy discussed by Sandra Blair in Chapter 4 in which police departments, district attorneys, and social service agencies retain advocates who can explain to a woman in a realistic and helpful manner what her rights are, what her options are, what the difficulties and advantages of each option are, and who will further help the woman implement the option of her choice.

We need to change the structure of social service agencies which make it so hard for a woman to get housing, financial assistance, or other types of aid that she decides to return home (or never leave) because the solutions seem more difficult than the problem.

And on a larger scale we need to change the entire acceptance of violence in this society through an increased examination of both our public media and our public educational systems. We MUST stop joking about and portraying violence in such a way that it gains implicit approval.

Finally, I submit that when we change the attitudes of men regarding violence toward women and enlist their all-out support in informing their male peers that battering is neither funny nor acceptable, we will move a lot further, a lot faster. It is well recognized that peers have a faster and greater effect on each of us than do nonpeers. It thus becomes imperative that we work with men who will work with other men if we are to stop battering.

Legal Solutions

We recognize the danger police officers walk into when they respond to domestic violence calls, and we must train them regarding how best to protect themselves in addition to educating them on the dangers and conflicts in which battered women find themselves. It is true that police officers die during domestic disturbances; it is also true that women die both during and following such beatings. It could be argued that police officers contract for a dangerous job when they enter law enforcement, but women do not contract to be battered when they enter marriage. In light of the earlier discussion regarding the interrelationships among the several legal arms of this country, education of police officers must happen simultaneously with training and education of district attorneys, judges, and legislators.

In addition to education and training, the public must begin demanding that domestic violence be taken seriously by those in law enforcement: police officers must make appropriate arrests; district attorneys must learn how to take these cases to court and win; judges must give reasonable sentences to men convicted of battering; and legislators must work with both law enforcement personnel and women's advocates to write new and effective legislation regarding programs, civil law, and criminal law which police, district attorneys, and judges can then implement.

The entire issue of temporary restraining orders (TROs), which is discussed by Eva Jefferson Paterson in Chapter 3, needs to be unraveled. We must teach women what TROs are and how to appropriately use them; we need to convince judges to issue TROs in a manner which can be effectively implemented by law enforcement; we need to work with police officers in outlining how and when they might enforce TROs; and we need to consider the computerization of TROs in the same manner as traffic tickets so that police officers can find out immediately if such an order remains in effect when they are asked to enforce one.

If either current or new laws are not being implemented by persons within the legal system, women must be willing to use litigation as a last resort. Two recent cases—one against the New York City Police Department and the New York City Family Court System and one in Alameda County, California, against the Oakland Police Department—have brought problems and complaints of women to the attention of police departments who had earlier refused to enforce the law in a way that protected battered women.[42] Although it may not be the best option, Eva Jefferson Paterson discusses these two court cases in Chapter 3 and points out that litigation should not be overlooked if other methods fail.

Legislation must not be forgotten. This, as Sandra Blair points out in Chapter 4, is where the "program laws" come from. In the 1978 Congress there were three major bills relating to battered women.[43] Each of these bills proposed allocation of monies for programs and information networks for battered women. Many states have also introduced bills to develop shelters, hot lines, mandatory reporting, protocol for reporting battering, and many other useful programs. It is important that we work with legislators to pass new laws and then work with police, district attorneys, and judges to implement those laws. It is equally important, however, to recognize that we must educate all four groups regarding the problems of battered women. If these people (most of them male) do not take the issues seriously, they are not likely either to write or pass legislation or to implement it once it has been passed.

Personal/Psychological Solutions

Most of the solutions in this section, although psychological and personal, cannot be initiated by the women and men involved in battering relationships. They must be set up so that battered women and their batterers can receive them at least initially from other people.

We must work both with women and men in violent homes to help them raise the level of their self-esteem. Since an overwhelming characteristic of both partners seems to be a low level of self-esteem, we must devise means of helping each person realize that she/he is worthy of higher self-regard and better treatment from her/his partner. We need to teach women that they can, indeed, survive on their own if they choose to leave the home, and that if they choose to remain within the home that they are worthy of better treatment. We need to teach men that beating their partner is not a sign of masculinity.

Second, we must teach both men and women alternative ways of relating to each other. This should be done, as Lenore Walker indicates in Chapter 2, while the partners are living apart.

Third, we must teach both partners to redefine acceptable sex-role behavior for both men and women. We must help them understand that it is not a man's prerogative to beat his wife, and it is not a woman's duty to stand by her man no matter how he treats her.

We must let each woman know that she is not the only one to experience such violence and we must offer her shelter, financial assistance, and personal support. She must know that the physical beatings and the psychological responses she is experiencing are shared by many others. Further, we might provide her with role models of women who have successfully escaped violent homes so that she can see that leaving is possible and that there is a chance for survival outside her violent surroundings.

We must teach women who choose to stay in the abusive home how to best protect themselves and what their legal rights are if and when they choose to take action against their partner or to leave the home. In other words, we must support women who choose to remain within their homes even if we do not agree with their decisions or if their decision frightens us.

We must work with women who have chosen to arrest and charge their men with assault. They need strength and support in following through with their court cases if district attorneys and police officers are no longer to have the excuse that "she won't follow through with it anyway, so we won't arrest or charge the man."

And finally, we need to work with people who are working with battered women: the police officers, the district attorneys, the counselors, the shelter workers, welfare workers, ministers, and others. We need to teach them how most appropriately to be of assistance to a woman who is experiencing such terror. In Chapter 2 Lenore Walker addresses this need to teach such helpers to be effective.

Using This Book

Within this book we have attempted to provide an overview
of the problem of battering, some solutions, a psychological
analysis, a legal analysis, and some strategies for developing
an advocacy system for battered women. We have also shared
some research on people's attitudes about battering. The
appendices should prove useful for further directed reading
and for initiating courses of action within each community
to help battered women. The book is not a complete picture
of battering—rather it is a beginning.

I hope that, whether choosing to read the entire book or
simply to select one or more chapters for perusing, the reader
will become more informed about battering. More importantly, however, I would hope that we could engage the
reader's interest and concern so that she/he will become not
just one of the more educated but one of the active problem
solvers on the issue of battered women. We would all be
pleased to have everyone join the complex struggle to end
marital violence.

1

WHAT KEEPS A WOMAN CAPTIVE IN A VIOLENT RELATIONSHIP?
The Social Context of Battering

Del Martin

Introduction

I would like to begin with excerpts from a letter a friend received from a battered wife:

> I am in my thirties and so is my husband. I have a high school diploma and am presently attending a local college, trying to obtain the additional education I need. My husband is a college graduate and a professional in his field. We are both attractive and, for the most part, respected and well-liked. We have four children and live in a middle-class home with all the comforts we could possibly want.
>
> I have everything, except life without fear.
>
> For most of my married life I have been periodically beaten by my husband. What do I mean by "beaten"? I mean that parts of my body have been hit violently and repeatedly, and that painful bruises, swelling, bleeding wounds, unconsciousness, and combinations of these things have resulted.
>
> Beating should be distinguished from all other kinds of physical abuse—including being hit and shoved around. When

I say my husband threatens me with abuse I do not mean he warns me that he may lose control. I mean that he shakes a fist against my face or nose, makes punching-bag jabs at my shoulder, or makes similar gestures which may quickly turn into a full-fledged beating.

I have had glasses thrown at me. I have been kicked in the abdomen when I was visibly pregnant. I have been kicked off the bed and hit while lying on the floor—again, while I was pregnant. I have been whipped, kicked and thrown, picked up again and thrown down again. I have been punched and kicked in the head, chest, face and abdomen more times than I can count.

I have been slapped for saying something about politics, for having a different view about religion, for swearing, for crying, for wanting to having intercourse.

I have been threatened when I wouldn't do something he told me to do. I have been threatened when he's had a bad day and when he's had a good day.

Now, the first response to this story, which I myself think of, will be "Why didn't you seek help?"

I did. Early in our marriage I went to a clergyman who, after a few visits, told me that my husband meant no real harm, that he was just confused and felt insecure. I was encouraged to be more tolerant and understanding. Most important, I was told to forgive him the beatings just as Christ has forgiven me from the Cross. I did that, too.

Things continued. Next time I turned to a doctor. I was given little pills to relax me and told to take things a little easier. I was just too nervous.

I turned to a friend, and when her husband found out, he accused me of either making things up or exaggerating the situation. She was told to stay away from me. She didn't, but she could no longer really help me. Just by believing me she was made to feel disloyal.

I turned to a professional family guidance agency. I was told there that my husband needed help and that I should find a way to control the incidents. I couldn't control the beatings—that was the whole point of my seeking help. At the agency I found I had to defend myself against the suspicion that I wanted to be hit, that I invited the beatings. Good God! Did the Jews invite themselves to be slaughtered in Germany?

I did go to two more doctors. One asked me what I had done to provoke my husband. The other asked if we had made up yet.

I called the police one time. They not only did not respond to the call, they called several hours later to ask if things had "settled down." I could have been dead by then!

I have nowhere to go if it happens again. No one wants to take in a woman with four children. Even if there were someone kind enough to care, no one wants to become involved in what is commonly referred to as a "domestic situation."

Everyone I have gone to for help has somehow wanted to blame me and vindicate my husband. I can see it lying there between their words and at the end of their sentences. The clergyman, the doctor, the counselor, my friend's husband, the police—all of them have found a way to vindicate my husband.

No one has to "provoke" a wife-beater. He will strike out when he's ready and for whatever reason he has at the moment.

I may be his excuse, but I have never been the reason.

I know that I do not want to be hit. I know, too, that I will be beaten again unless I can find a way out for myself and my children. I am terrified for them also.

As a married woman I have no recourse but to remain in the situation which is causing me to be painfully abused. I have suffered physical and emotional battering and spiritual rape because the social structure of my world says I cannot do anything about a man who wants to beat me. . . . But staying with my husband means that my children must be subjected to the emotional battering caused when they see their mother's beaten face or hear her screams in the middle of the night.

I know that I have to get out. But when you have nowhere to go, you know that you must go on your own and expect no support. I have to be ready for that. I have to be ready to support myself and the children completely, and still provide a decent environment for them. I pray that I can do that before I am murdered in my own home.[1]

Unfortunately, that is a rather typical story. The problem is that wife battering becomes significant in terms of public support only when it can be proven that it affects millions of people and is not merely a few isolated cases. Consequently, many of us are forced to play the numbers game in order to make the public aware that wife abuse is indeed a very serious social problem.

Data Gathering Problems

Definitions

Accurately determining the incidence of wife beating, of course, is next to impossible. Not only because obvious sources of statistics such as police, court, doctors, social workers, and mental health professionals do not keep such records but also because of differences in defining the problem.

The police term *domestic disturbance* is not synonymous with wife beating. A domestic disturbance may or may not involve any physical violence. Even agreeing on the definition of violence poses a problem. Police seem to think that few domestic disturbances are really serious. They tend to define violence in terms of its effect. In the absence of blood or visible injury, they are apt to discount the wife's report of her husband's brutality. The law defines violence by the degree of its severity and social scientists tend to measure violence by the degree of its acceptance. The fact that one-fifth of American adults in a Harris Poll approved of slapping one's spouse on appropriate occasions has been seen by social scientists as legitimizing a certain amount of violence.[2]

Language of Reporting:
The Case of the Missing Gender

Another problem in gathering statistics on wife beating, besides the fact that it is one of the most unreported crimes in this country,[3] is the language in police reports and research studies which often describes assailants and victims in non-specific terms. Gender is omitted. Although many have rebeled against feminist attempts to desex the language, suddenly it becomes vogue when discussing domestic violence.

The Kansas City, Missouri, Police Study of 1971-1972 refers to victims and suspects without specifying either their sex or marital roles.[4] Social scientists speak of "family" violence and "intrafamily" murder or violence between "spouses." It should be made clear that what we are discussing here is the battering of women by the men they love and live with, whether or not they are legally married. Admittedly, psychological abuse of women is every bit as devastating and may be even more prevalent, but my remarks will be limited here to physical abuse.

What Some of the Data Say

A national survey of 2,143 couples randomly selected and demographically representative was conducted in 1976 by sociologists Murray Straus, Suzanne Steinmetz, and Richard Gelles[5] to measure the magnitude of marital violence. From the results, Straus estimates that of the approximately 47 million couples living together in the United States in 1975, over 1.7 million had faced a husband or wife wielding a knife or gun; more than 2 million were beaten up by the spouse and another 2 1/2 million had engaged in high-risk injury violence. The findings showed a high rate of violence for wives, but the data did not indicate what proportion of violent acts committed by the wives were in self-defense. Husbands showed a higher rate for the most dangerous and injurious forms of violence, beatings or using a knife or gun, and for the repetitiveness of their brutal acts.

Wives reportedly resort to violence mostly as a protective reaction, in self-defense or out of fear. Fighting back, they say, often results in even more severe beatings. Lenore Walker, who details a three-phase cycle theory of marital violence, says that many wives, when they recognize the inevitability of an acute incident, may deliberately provoke it in order to get it over with and move on to the next stage, a calm, loving, respite stage.[6]

The practice of wife beating crosses all boundaries of economic class, race, national origin, or educational background. It happens in the ghetto, in working class neighborhoods, in middle-class homes, and in the wealthiest counties of our nation. The often-held assumption that violence occurs more frequently among lower-class families could be due to variations in reporting.[7] Having fewer resources and less privacy, these families are more apt to call police or seek the services of other public agencies. Middle- or upper-class wives or husbands have greater access to private support services and thus are less apt to come to the attention of authorities.

Women who are treated for physical injuries or for severe depression are often victims who go undetected, since they do not volunteer the information, out of fear or shame, and few doctors ask. One psychiatrist who claimed he had never encountered a case of marital violence in his practice was challenged to ask his next 10 female clients. Eight out of the 10 proved to be victims.

Elaine Hilberman and Kit Munson, in their study of 60 women drawn from a rural health clinic, found that the history of physical abuse was known by the clinicians in only 4 of the 60 cases, although most of the women and their children had received ongoing medical care at that clinic.[8] A doctor who treats a battered woman's wounds and sends her back home to be beaten again may be exercising a kind of professional detachment, but he is also ignoring responsibility for what may be society's only contact with a lonely woman who needs help.

The danger in our inability to identify victims is that violence unchecked often leads to murder. The Kansas City Police Study showed that 40% of the homicides in that city in 1971 were cases of spouse killing spouse. In 85% of these cases, the police had been called in at least once prior to the homicide and in almost 50% of these cases police had been summoned five or more times within a two-year period before the murder occurred.

The husband in domestic homicides is almost as often the victim as is the wife. Since a woman does not have the physical strength of a man, she may, out of desperation to put a stop to the beating, pick up the nearest object which may turn out to be a lethal weapon. In the last year, the news media have reported a sizable number of trials in which the wife murdered her husband after years of being subjected to constant beatings.

One of the most telling statistics regarding the number of battered women in this country is the fact that whenever a shelter for battered women is established, whether it be in an urban area or rural area, it is filled to capacity immediately and there is a long waiting list. This says that not only are there a lot of battered women out there but also that they will seek help as soon as it becomes available.

Social science, as it is practiced, does not apply to women at all, according to Gene Errington.[9] She says, "We are silenced. We do not form the thoughts or the concepts which govern our lives and the way in which we see the world. Our experience is never adequately described by the disciplines in the social sciences. We always end up the objects of the study. We are told here are some people that we will look at from this particular position, and the position we are being looked at as women is one that we do not occupy."

There are social scientists who are speculating on what makes the difference between the man who merely wounds his wife and the man who kills her. One researcher sees the murderer as the man who has less experience at violence, who can go too far when he loses control. Another says that alcohol could affect the judgment of a man regarding the degree of battering a woman could take without dying.[10]

Most research into the cause of marital violence concentrates on external influences of the husband's behavior. He was under stress, he lost his job, he drank too much, his mother had an extramarital affair. Whatever the rationalization, it serves to excuse the husband's behavior and remove his responsibility for his own acts. The wife's condition is not seen in its totality, but only in terms of what she may have said or done to provoke her husband's anger. The triggering of violent incidents is almost always trivial (for example, she wore her hair in a pony tail, she prepared a casserole instead of fresh meat for dinner, she said she did not like the pattern of the wallpaper). In no way do any of these events warrant a violent response. Even if the woman did provoke her husband's anger, there can be no justification for these severe beatings. Furthermore, any approach that attempts to change the wife's behavior, in order to change the husband's behavior, only further victimizes her.

Understanding Social Imperatives

The sheer number of violent male/female relationships indicates that we would be foolhardy to regard domestic violence solely in terms of the personal interaction between two people. In order to understand why it is happening, we must also recognize the social imperatives that influence husband and wife behavior. This includes a review of sex-role socialization, marriage, the criminal justice system, and the response of other helping agencies in times of crisis. All of these factors have a powerful influence in what we usually think of as a private and very personal relationship.

Sex-Role Socialization

The roles of wife and husband did not grow out of biological reality or necessity, but were arbitrarily set to preserve the patriarchy. Concepts of masculinity (strong, active, rational, aggressive, authoritarian) and feminity (submissive, passive, dependent, weak, masochistic) were adopted by men who seized power in the family and society with the advent of monogamous marriage. The roles were mandated by the unwritten marriage contract and incorporated into the culture by church and state. Jean Baker Miller says that dominant groups usually define acceptable roles for subordinates, which typically involve providing services the dominant group does not wish to perform for itself. Functions that the dominant group wishes to perform are carefully guarded and closed to subordinates who are usually said to be unable to perform them, because of innate defects or deficiencies of mind or body, therefore, immutable and impossible of change or development.[11] An apt illustration is the 1944 Florida Supreme Court decision which describes a woman's legal status in the following way: "A woman's responsibilities and faculties remain intact from age of maturity until she finds her mate, whereupon incompetency seizes her and she needs protection in an extreme degree. Upon the advent of widowhood, she is reinstated with all of her capabilities which have been dormant during the marriage, only to lose them again upon remarriage."[12] Miller also points out that if subordinates adopt the characteristics assigned to them, they are considered well-adjusted. This is the means by which the dominant group legitimizes the unequal relationship; incorporates it into cultural values, morality, and social structure; and thereby obscures the true nature of the relationship—that is, the existence of inequality.

The Broverman study in which professional therapists were asked to describe typical male and female behavior, as well as that of normal adult behavior, sex unspecified, is a classic example of this technique.[13] Not surprisingly, the therapists described male and female behavior in stereotypical terms and equated the normal adult with commonly accepted male characteristics. Thus, both males and females could be labeled "unhealthy" by mental health professionals if they exhibit nonstereotypic behavior.

Ruth Pancoast and Linda Weston point out that men experience no dichotomy between adulthood and manhood because society says the two are identical; but the woman who tries to be a healthy adult does so at the expense of being unfeminine, and the woman who adjusts to her "normal" role, does so at the expense of being a healthy adult. Society has thus constructed a no-win situation for women.[14]

Donald Moreland says we must recognize that virtually all men are angry at women. The man who batters is acting out in an extreme what most men feel, at least part of the time. He attributes men's anger toward women to the repression of emotion in men, the limitation of intimacy only with women, and to the socialization of men to be powerful. He warns, "Given the few number of men who really get to exercise power and the fact that we are all socialized to be powerful, there are a lot of us walking around who are pent up volcanoes ready to explode." Together, he says, we need to break down the impossible image of masculinity, which dooms men to feelings of frustration and rage and puts women in the role of men's targets.[15]

Marriage

Wife beating is not a new phenomenon. It probably began with the emergence of the first monogamous pairing relationship and the patriarchal social and economic system. Prior to the pairing marriage, women as the only discernible parents were held in high esteem among the clans. The new arrangement came about because women sought protection from open season on rape and because men wanted to authenticate their identity and rights as fathers. The cost to women for their husband's so-called protection from other males came very high. The new father right brought about the complete subjugation of one sex by the other.[16] Although polygamy and infidelity remained men's privileges, the strictest fidelity was demanded of women who were regarded as their husband's property. Women were confined to certain parts of the home, isolated, guarded, and restricted from public activity. A woman was duty bound to marry, satisfy her husband's lust, bear his children, and tend to his household. If she showed any signs of a will of her own, the husband was expected by both church and state to chastise her for her transgression. Women were burned at the stake under many pretexts, including scolding and nagging, refusing to have intercourse, and miscarrying, even though the miscarriage was caused by a kick or a blow from the husband.[17]

Instead of asking the all-too-frequent question, "Why does a woman stay in a violent marriage?" we should be asking "What is it about marriage in this society that keeps a woman captive in a violent marriage?".

Barbara Hirsch describes marriage as a contract entered into by three parties: the husband, the wife, and the state.[18] The power in the relationship is not divided equally. The state maintains the controlling interest, the husband has authority in the home, and the wife serves at the pleasure of both. The state's exclusive jurisdiction over the marriage has a tremendous effect on husband and wife behavior. The marriage contract is unlike most contracts. Lenore Weitzman points out, "Its provisions are unwritten, its penalties are unspecified and the terms of the contract are typically unknown to the contracting parties. Prospective spouses are neither informed of the terms of the contract, nor are they allowed any options about these terms."[19] Implicit in the unwritten contract is the early English common law "By marriage, the husband and wife are one person in law. The very being or legal existence of the woman is suspended during the marriage, or at least is incorporated and consolidated into that of the husband, under whose wing, protection and cover, she performs everything."[20]

In marriage the woman loses her personhood. She is identified in terms of her husband. Legally he is head of the household and responsible for supporting the family; she is the subordinate and responsible for housework, child care, and other nurturance. With few exceptions, the wife takes her husband's name, his domicile, and becomes his legal dependent. She must literally "love, honor, and obey"—or suffer the consequences. Her labor is a duty to be performed without value or compensation. In many states the husband has exclusive authority over community property, including all of the wife's earnings, and can dissipate the family assets without the wife's prior knowledge or consent. The wages earned by the husband belong to him, and the wife is totally dependent upon his whim or generosity. It is particularly important here to point out that this legal, state-enforced contract exists even in those marriages in which the partners attempt to set up equalized relationships and that the state's contractual rights always supersede any agreement between the spouses.

Needless to say, the expectations women have about marriage differ significantly from the reality of the marriage contract. In a study on the reasons why men and women marry, women's chief motives stemmed from the desire to get out from under parental control and "be free." They also married because of the consequences of not marrying. The men's reasons for marrying were more in keeping with the interest of the state. Marriage should incorporate fatherhood and provide the man with a companion to do the housework, take care of his sexual needs, and look after the children.[21]

Jessie Bernard says two separate marriages exist: his and hers. For centuries men have railed against marriage as a trap set for them by scheming women who were trying to gain protection and security, but it seems to work in the opposite way. Of marriage, Bernard states "Men have cursed it, aimed barbed witticisms at it, degraded it, bemoaned it, and never ceased to want and need it or profit from it." Research shows that marriage has positive effects on a man's mental health, his career earning power, his longevity, his happiness, and his comfort. Women, on the other hand, do not fare as well. Many suffer from severe states of depression. The bride who was catered to before marriage, becomes the caterer after marriage. She must actively accommodate herself to suit her husband's expectations. Often she reshapes, adapts, adjusts, or represses her personality to keep the marrige intact. Many women make full-time careers of protecting the self-image of their husbands. Failure of the marriage in patriarchal society means the wife's personal failure as a woman.[22]

Though we may try to deny it, the feudal system of marriage is still in existence today. Aaron Rutledge says that despite the age of jets and satellites, some people try to get along on a horse-and-buggy marriage. Individuals who would not tolerate a feudal society still insist upon an owner/dependent type of family structure.[23]

With the exception of South Dakota, Oregon, and Nebraska, rape is not recognized as a crime when it occurs within marriage. By early common law, a husband has sexual title to his wife: the absolute right to have sex with her, even if it is against her will, or if it means sexual violence. While rape is a commonly acknowledged form of wife abuse, most state laws explicitly exempt husbands from prosecution for this behavior. The law granting a man access to his wife's body does not even protect the wife who is separated from her husband but who has not yet received her divorce decree. Technically she is still married to him. Even though she has established her own domicile, her husband is legally entitled to access to the premises and to her person.

Some legislators are willing to go so far as to make rape a crime when the couple has separated and are maintaining separate domiciles, but not when they are still living together. They argue that vindictive wives may bring false charges against their husbands, but the fact remains that the rules of evidence placing the burden of proof on the complainant would still hold for this crime, just as it does for all others. If husbands were no longer exempted from rape laws, there probably would not be a great increase in prosecutions. Adherents of law reform see it more as a deterrent or educational tool—a statement that sexual assault of wives will no longer be accepted by society. As it is now, a man can rape his wife with impunity and with state approval.

The problem with existing marriage and divorce laws, according to Lenore Weitzman, is that they "favor structure, stability and security to the exclusion of flexibility, change and individual freedom."[24] Roles which the courts presently demand of husbands and wives are rigid, archaic, and arbitrary. The acting out of these roles—the authoritarian husband and the servile wife—and the imbalance of power they represent are largely responsible for marital conflicts.

Balance of power has long been a principle of international relations to prevent strong industrialized nations from taking over or victimizing weaker, underdeveloped countries and to stave off war. By analogy, creating a balance of power, both economic and social, between marital partners could be the means of preventing one sex from taking advantage of the other and preventing the violence this imbalance provokes. Seen in this light, marrige would be a partnership, an egalitarian relationship in which both husband and wife have equal ownership and share management and control of the income, assets, and liabilities. To effect such a partnership, marriage laws would have to be redefined to allow the individuals involved to determine and agree upon their own particular needs and lifestyles. One standard provision, without any option, which I would like to see written into every marriage contract is the restraining order: recognition at the outset by both parties that violence will not be tolerated in the relationship and that violation will automatically make the offender subject to arrest and prosecution.

The Criminal Justice System

Historical Laws

Too numerous to mention are the worldwide accounts of the cruel and barbarous treatment of women in the name of the law, religion, and social custom—treatment that clearly indicates how entrenched sexual inequality, at the least, and woman-hating, at the extreme, is in human history.

Peter the Great introduced some reforms in Russia during the late seventeenth century allowing women to attend public gatherings, requiring individual consent before marriage, and giving married women the right to full ownership and control over their own property.[25] In England the law was changed in the 1800s to allow a wife who had been habitually beaten by her husband to the point of "endangering her life" to separate from him, though not to divorce him. A British husband was also prohibited from selling his wife into prostitution, but only if she was under 16 years of age.[26]

In our own country a husband was permitted to beat his wife so long as he did not use a switch any bigger around than his thumb. In 1874, the North Carolina Supreme Court nullified the husband's right to chastise his wife under any circumstances, but the court's ruling became ambiguous when it added, "If no permanent injury has been inflicted nor malice, cruelty, nor dangerous violence shown by the husband, it is better to draw the curtain, shut out the public gaze and leave the parties to forgive and forget."[27] The latter qualifying statement has become the basis of the American legal system.

Laws against assault and battery, in this country, are rarely invoked against husbands because the criminal justice system (which is male dominated) and victims of domestic violence (who are primarily females) differ in their interpretations of "serious injury, malice, cruelty and danger."

Police

Police often say they are called out of vindictiveness. The caller tries to use the police as a counterpunch and get an authority figure to take her side in an argument. Police officers feel they neither have the time, competence, nor social mandate to deal with domestic disputes. Such calls thus receive a low priority.

In a sample of 283 calls over a two-month period in Vancouver, British Columbia, it was found that a car was dispatched 53.8% of the time for man/woman fights. In only 10% of the cases did these calls receive priority one attention. If the caller mentioned violence plus weapons and alcohol, the probability went up to 67%, and if children were involved then it went up to 73%. The decision of whether or not to dispatch a police car was not based on the availability of personnel or vehicles, because the dispatch rate did not fluctuate with the time of day or day of the week. The arrest rate in this study was about 7%.[28]

The reluctance of police to make arrests is a common complaint of wife-victims. When a woman calls the police, it is an act of desperation. She expects immediate response and protection. At most, the officer, if and when he does show up, may get the husband to leave the home for a cooling-off period. Police, of course, can only make felony arrests on probable cause and must witness the event in order to make an arrest for an assault and battery misdemeanor. The responsibility then is on the victim to make a citizen's arrest, but she may not be aware of that right and police may not inform her of the right to make the arrest herself. Additionally, she may be in a state of trauma, having just been beaten, and incapable of making that decision or fearful of reprisal if she is the one to initiate criminal proceedings against her husband. Should she be insistent upon her right to have her assailant arrested, the wife-victim is likely to be discouraged from doing so by the police.

At the training academy in Michigan, officers are told to avoid arrests and to appeal to the woman's vanity. They are told to explain the whole procedure of obtaining a warrant, that she is going to have to sign it and appear in court and should consider the loss of time and court costs, and that victims usually change their minds before going to court, and perhaps she really ought to postpone any decision about making an arrest.[29]

The training bulletin of the Oakland, California, Police Department warns of the dangers to the officer if he arrests the husband, who is apt to turn on him "to save face in front of his family." The bulletin also states that when no serious crime has been committed, but one of the parties demands arrest, the officer should explain the ramifications, such as loss of wages and bail procedure, and encourage the parties "to reason together."[30] This policy has made the Oakland Police Department the defendants in a suit brought in Federal Court by four battered women on the grounds that the non-arrest policy is a denial of their rights to equal protection under the law and a breach of the duty of the police to make arrests.

A similar suit is pending before the Manhattan Supreme Court, not only against the New York Police Department but also against the clerk and probation employees in Family Court. This suit was brought by 12 battered women and 59 more have filed affidavits—a clear indication that many victims would follow through on their complaints if the criminal justice system were responsive and less obstructive in its procedures.

One incident cited in the class action complaint against the New York police shows that even when an officer witnesses the crime and is thus authorized to make the arrest, he may refuse to do so. According to the complaint, the neighbors called the police and when they arrived the fight was still going on. The officers had to pry the man's fingers from around his wife's neck. The neighbors shouted, "Arrest him, he's going to kill her!". The officers shrugged and said they could not interfere with domestic fights and left.

Family crisis intervention training for police has been highly touted as a means of handling domestic violence cases. The concept sounds impressive but the effectiveness, solution-wise, is questionable. The officers are taught how to break up the fight, calm down the parties involved, mediate the dispute, and make referrals to counseling. While a reduction in repeat calls is attributed to this training, it may be that victims do not call back because they feel it would be useless to do so.

Most police crisis intervention training guides refer to family disputes, but rarely make direct reference to wife beating. I did manage to find one single example, which discussed a married couple who had an argument resulting in the wife's nose being broken by her husband. The officer asked the wife for her story, asked if she wanted her husband arrested, if she still loved her husband, and where he could find the husband. After locating the husband the officer informed him that his wife was in pain, asked him if he loved his wife, and what had happened. He then brought the two together and asked them to talk and to apologize to each other. He reminded them that their child would never forget incidents such as the present one and suggested that if they began to argue they should remember their responsibilities and one of them should leave. He pointed out that they were lucky this time—the husband had no charges brought against him; the wife had *only* a broken nose. The officer left.[31]

The benevolent nonarrest policy might be satisfactory in some instances if the husband assailant responded to leniency by resolving never to resort to violence again. Unfortunately, it does not work that way. The man is more apt to see this leniency as reinforcement for his abusive behavior. He quickly learns that lesser injuries such as a broken nose are tolerated by the system and the probability of his being taken into custody is remote.

Equally disconcerting is the following reference in the training guide published by the Law Enforcement Assistance Foundation of the U.S. Department of Justice: "Although the prevailing American culture tolerates a minimum of physical force as a reaction to anger, such physical force is a common response among certain ethnic groups. Therefore, whether or not the use of such force can be considered serious depends in part on the cultural background of the people using it. In some cultures, the dominance of the father is especially noticeable. In Puerto Rican families for example, the need to assert masculinity, machismo, is very important to males and taught to them early."[32] Such an approach not only reflects some racist assumptions but if, in fact, some communities are more tolerant of wife beating that situation is part of the problem and should not obviate enforcement of the law. The values and perceptions that become the excuse for doing nothing are those of patriarchal cultures and do not necessarily reflect the perception of women who are victims of both the sub-culture and the dominant American culture.

Much of the crisis intervention training is geared toward teaching officers how to protect themselves—and rightfully so. The FBI statistics for 1974 showed that one out of five officers killed in the line of duty died trying to break up a family fight.[33] Yet, ironically, police still dismiss domestic disturbances as mere family "spats." I submit that if they are dangerous to trained police officers, they must certainly be dangerous to defenseless women and their children.

District Attorneys

Male prosecutors react in much the same way as police. District Attorneys count stitches and witnesses before deciding if they have a winning case. In San Francisco the District Attorney was challenged to practice on some of these cases so he might learn how to win them. A couple of months after the challenge was made I received a letter that was directed to the police chief by an assistant district attorney praising a police officer who had investigated the case so well that the assistant district attorney had been able to win it.

Sgt. Barry Whalley, of the Oakland Police Department, told me in a personal interview that the odds of a marital violence case ever reaching the courtroom are about 100 to 1. Deputy Chief James Bannon, of the Detroit Police Department, said that in 1972, in Detroit, there were 4,900 domestic assaults which had survived the screening process long enough to at least have a warrant prepared and the complainant referred to the assault and battery squad. Through the process of conciliation, complainant harrassment, and prosecutorial discretion, however, fewer than 300 of these cases were ultimately tried by a court of law. In most of these, the court used the judicial process to conciliate rather than adjudicate.[34]

Judges

Once a wife-victim reaches the courtroom, she finds that even though the judge finds the husband guilty, the judge is likely to let him off with a warning, a suspended sentence, probation, or a small fine on his promise that he will not do it again. The classic example was the case in New York City in which a woman brought charges against her former common-law husband for beating her savagely on five different occasions within 1½ years. Although she had been beaten so severely that she had been hospitalized on at least two of the occasions, had lost an eye and part of an ear, her assailant was released each time on his promise to the judge that he would not repeat the offense.[35] I am told that the victim finally solved the situation herself; she committed suicide.

Social Service Agencies

Social service agencies are also often not effective in offering battered wives help and protection. They are not open at night or on weekends when the violence usually occurs. Emergency housing for women with children, until recently, was virtually nonexistent. A 1973 survey in Los Angeles showed that there were 4,000 beds available for men, but only 30 for women and children and none for mothers with sons over four years of age.[36]

A woman who flees from a violent home in the middle of the night is usually without funds and often has only the clothes on her back. If she seeks welfare she may be turned down because her husband's salary disqualifies her. Unless she has filed for divorce or has established separate maintenance, technically she is neither homeless nor destitute. In St. Louis, Missouri, I am told, it takes from four to six weeks for the first welfare check to arrive. Without a place to go or means of support until she can become independent, the wife-victim is often forced to return to her violent husband.

A study of 100 battered wives in England revealed that 89 had fled their homes, 36 had fled 4 or more times, and some had left 10 or even 20 times. They had returned home because: (1) they were found by their husband, who either threatened them with further abuse or promised to reform, or (2) none of the agencies they turned to for help could offer them protection or a roof over their head. Also, many of the women married right out of high school and had no job, experience, or marketable skills.[37]

If a woman manages to get away and obtain a divorce, she still has no guarantee of safety. Some ex-husbands continue to stalk and hunt down "their women" for years after a divorce, forcing their victims to move and change jobs continually. In spite of this danger, judges continue to grant violent fathers visitation rights and thus the opportunity to further intimidate their ex-wives.

When a woman concludes that her husband is not going to change, that she has no alternative but to leave him, she is forced to face the cold hard facts of the poverty of her existence. How many times have you heard that a wife is one man away from welfare? How is she going to support herself and her children? Even if she has worked before marrying, her lack of recent references counts against her. In all likelihood, she will have to take a menial job, at low pay, to reestablish herself as a member of the work force. Discrimination against women in employment often precludes her from advancement in position and salary. Despite myths to the contrary, studies show that alimony is rarely awarded and most fathers do not even make child support payments as ordered by the court. In the first year after divorce, 62% of fathers fail to comply fully with court-ordered child support and 42% do not make a single payment.[38] Without child support, or child care, the divorced working mother may find her take-home pay is less than the minimal subsistence offered by welfare.

Adult Violence: A Cultural Perspective

James W. Prescott contends that major causes of adult violence are the deprivation of physical affection as children and the repression of female sexuality. He also claims that while we relate the biological with the social or cultural influences on violent behavior, we must also examine philosophical religious value systems which determine the morality of physical sensory pleasure. Prescott believes there is a reciprocal relationship between pleasure and violence in that the presence of one inhibits the other. When the brain's pleasure circuits are on, the violence circuits are off, and vice versa.[39]

Prescott tested his hypothesis that deprivation of physical pleasure results in physical violence by examining cross-cultural studies of childrearing practices, sexual behaviors, and physical violence. He found that societies which lavished affection upon infants had low religious activity and less crime and violence among adults. He also found that societies in which there was low infant indulgence were more likely to practice slavery and polygamy and fear of an aggressive God. Societies which punish premarital and extramarital sex are likely to engage in wife purchasing, worship of an authoritarian God, emphasis on morality, the practice of slavery, and to have a high incidence of crime and violence.

From these studies, Prescott contends that the origins of the fundamental reciprocal relationship between physical violence and physical pleasure can be traced to philosophical dualism in the theology of body-soul relationships. The Judeo-Christian concept of sex as evil and as an impediment to the ultimate goal—saving the soul—and the equating of men with spirit and women with evil or sex has had a deep and negative influence on American society, which is a very violence-prone nation.

Solutions: Current Perspectives

So what can be done to alter this destructive collision course between men and women? Family crisis intervention training, victim/witness advocacy programs, emergency hotlines, shelters for battered women and their children, and couples therapy are all services that have been recently developed to deal with the immediate crisis. The shelter network established by grassroots women's groups, with its underground railway, by which battered women can be transported from one state to another, affords the only real protection to the victim. The other measures may stop a particular incident and postpone or reduce further violence, but do not prevent its recurrence.

The fact remains that wife beating is a crime. In Oregon the law was recently changed to make arrest mandatory, unless the victim seriously objected. The International Association of Chiefs of Police, which in 1974 supported the family crisis intervention policy of nonarrest, issued new training keys (245 and 246) in 1976 reiterating that wife beating should be treated as a crime, to be investigated and reported. The training keys also stated that unless the police do their job, despite protests from prosecutors and judges about crowded court calendars, nothing will change.

In Ohio a bill has been introduced to make a second offense of wife beating a felony, rather than a misdemeanor. An innovative judge in Hammond, Indiana, names the wife-victim her husband's probation officer, on the premise that the man would not hesitate to beat up his wife, but he might think twice about beating up an officer of the court.[40] In Milwaukee, Wisconsin, the first offender is required to participate in a treatment program or face prosecution. However, the charge is held open. A recurrence of violence results in two charges of battery, arrest, and advice to the court that the man has already been given informal probation and should therefore be dealt with more harshly.[41]

In Minnesota, a bill was passed allocating $600,000 for use in counteracting domestic violence: $100,000 for a displaced homemaker's program, $50,000 for public education about violence in the home, and the balance for refuges for battered women and their children. And in West Virginia, welfare regulations were recently modified to allow immediate emergency funds for battered women.

Women have been developing their own support systems for victims, based upon the concept of women helping women. They provide consciousness raising, assertiveness training, self-defense, and feminist therapy, if indeed therapy is called for. The support groups work to explore what part is the woman's responsibility and what is imposed upon her by society. The wife-victim becomes aware of the options open to her, knowing that whatever she chooses, she will have the support of other women.

What we also need are counterpart programs conducted by men—men who will work with battering husbands in much the same way as women are helping the wife-victims. If men would stop making jokes about wife beating, if they would let the batterers know unequivocally that beating up women is not acceptable male behavior, if men would offer husband offenders peer support and programs to help them change their destructive patterns, I think we would move a lot faster toward ending marital violence. Barry Shapiro, of the East Bay Men's Center in Berkeley, California, says that his and other men's groups affiliated with the National Conference on Men and Masculinity are considering the formation of such programs, and I understand that the Men's Center in Portland, Oregon, is already offering counseling services to batterers.

The long-range task, of course, is that of education and the elimination of sexism. The British Select Committee on Violence and Marriage made the recommendation that much more serious attention should be given within our school system to a program on domestic conflict. The committee suggested that the curriculum include the study of roles of the partners in marriage, their relationships with their children, laws surrounding family life, especially that relating to marriage, and instruction given about the use and value of social services.[42]

Summary

In summary, I offer another quote from Gene Errington: "Men beat their wives because they are permitted to do so and nobody stops them. Women are beaten because they are trained and forced and maintained into dependence and nobody helps them."

We need to look at short-term, emergency safety measures. For the long run, we face the challenge to envision a new society in which men and women can relate to each other in marriage and in society at large as equals. Wife beating is clearly an abuse of power.

2

HOW BATTERING HAPPENS AND
HOW TO STOP IT

Lenore E. Walker

It has become clear that despite most people's desire to live in a peaceful family, that is a goal never reached by many. Although the history of spouse abuse is ancient, it has never been adequately studied. Even today with all of the national interest in battered women, men, children, and other family members, government and private agencies concerned with allocating monies have not specifically designated domestic violence research as a top priority. Nor have monies to develop adequate treatment programs been widely disbursed.

Spouse abuse has been considered an acceptable resolution to marital disagreements, as long as violence is contained within the home. Talking about such assaults and reporting them to police or others in the helping professions has been a taboo, until the Women's Movement, using the technique of consciousness raising groups, was able to get women to share the pain and the horror of living within a home where they were being battered.

It is important to note that although we talk about spouse abuse, I am convinced that in 99 out of 100 cases, we are really talking about battered women. While it is no doubt true that some small percentage of men are being beaten by their women, the incidence, frequency, and severity is nowhere near the magnitude of the problem of wife abuse.

In early 1975, when I was a practicing psychologist on the faculty of Rutgers Medical School, several of my clients began to report physical and psychological abuse by the men with whom they had intimate relationships. With a feminist psychotherapeutic approach, these women were able to stop being a victim of such assaults. These early cases stimulated my curiosity and I began to ask my colleagues on the medical school and psychology faculties if they, too, were seeing women patients who were reporting similar psychological or physical abuse by their male partners. You can guess what they told me: "Not me, I haven't seen any such person." Then I would ask them if they had seen anybody who reports having any kind of injuries from those arguments? "Well," they said, "They were just involved in typical marital disputes." Such was the philosophy underlying treatment that psychologists and other professionals have been according victims of domestic abuse until recently. Slowly, with my urging and my persistence, these colleagues and those in the feminist network began to recognize and refer other such women to me.

When I moved to Denver in late 1975, I continued this research. I began the round of government funding agencies to support this work and was unable to find any kind of funding, until 1977. Nevertheless, I have pursued it and I want to share some of the psychological theories that I have been deducing from the stories that battered women have shared.

Development of treatment alternatives is hampered because we do not have a sufficient amount of information that describes the women and men who live in violence. Even though we are now working with many of these people, there still is not enough knowledge to compare batterers and battered women with other people who are also involved in violence. The isolation that has surrounded this particular crime has made it impossible for us to gain the information we need to begin to develop adequate treatment.

Let us look first at some statistics. Murray Straus, Richard Gelles, and Suzanne Steinmetz are sociologists who conducted the first epidemiological study by scientifically selecting a cross-section of people in this country and asking them on the telephone if they had experienced any domestic violence during that year.[1] Despite the inadequate methodology, they came up with an estimate that during the year of their study, 1975, 28% of all families in the population had experienced at least one physical battering incident. That is a lot of people. I estimate that as many as one out of every two women will suffer some form of violence against themselves at some time during their lives—again, a whole lot of people.

There is a strong relationship between wife abuse, child abuse, and incest.[2] The National Center for Child Abuse and Neglect estimates that in homes where there is known wife abuse and child abuse, the abusers are the male batterers. Normally, child abuse statistics show that 40% of the perpetrators of child abuse and neglect are the men in the home. In homes where the woman is not being battered, the mother commits approximately 60% of the child abuse. When the woman is being battered, the mother commits only 30% of the child abuse. This indicates the likelihood of the man behaving violently toward his entire family. Although these two forms of domestic violence may overlap, effective treatment strategies differ. If a battered woman is supported and helped to become more independent, then she can be expected to take effective charge of her life. Children, on the other hand, remain dependent on adults to meet most of their needs regardless of support systems for emotional independence.

I began interviewing battered women who volunteered to speak with me or the other project interviewers in 1975 and continued through 1978. Although the data were collected in an unstructured fashion, there were numerous similarities which appeared from case to case. I report them in detail in my book, *The Battered Woman*.[3] After the 120 in-depth interviews were completed, and about 300 more were done with battered women and their helpers, it was decided to begin collecting information about women victims of violence in a more systematic way. This new research, which began in July 1978, is being funded by the National Institute of Mental Health and is conducted under the auspices of the Battered Women Research Center located at the Colorado Women's College in Denver. When it is completed we will have statistical data for 400 battered women in the Rocky Mountain area.

Let me say a quick word about batterers. They tend not to be stereotypical of a criminal or psychopath. They are not necessarily mentally ill people. They come from all walks of life; they hold good positions in the community; they serve on our courts, in our police agencies, in our mental health institutions; they are our psychologists, as well as our lawyers, judges, and legislators. This makes it not only difficult to recognize a batterer but often difficult to believe when you meet him. It also makes it difficult for battered women to receive effective treatment from him if he, too, beats his own wife.

According to the women that I have interviewed, there is a very high incidence of child abuse and neglect in their batterer's history. Batterers are reported to come from families in which they were physically abused or emotionally neglected as children. This is not true for the battered woman. Interestingly enough, most of the battered women come from homes where they were treated like the stereotype of daddy's little girls. Approximately 80% were raised with very traditional sex-role socialization. These data suggest that such sex-role stereotyping in childhood is a major factor in determining the power relationship between men and women, which allows battering behavior to take place. When children are disciplined by being hit, they are taught that the person who loves them has the right to hurt them in order to teach them a lesson. It is also well-documented that the sex-role socialization lessons little girls learn are to be nurturing, compliant, and a good, passive wife and the lessons little boys learn are to be strong, aggressive, and the husband in charge. These early lessons set the stage upon which later violence is played out.

There is much to be learned from the stories of battered women. From my research I have developed a psychological rationale regarding why the battered woman becomes a victim, how the process of victimization further entraps her, and how the psychological paralysis which prevents her from leaving the relationship results. This psychological paralysis is the construct of learned helplessness, which develops from the sense of powerlessness that normal sex-role socialization provides. While any woman can accidentally find herself in a battering relationship, those who remain trapped in it suffer from further victimization. Understanding the maintenance of violent behavior, once it occurs, became a very imperative question, as I listened to these women's stories. While I know battering did not continue because either the men or the women liked it (the old masochism myth), the specifics of why a woman stayed in that relationship needed some kind of response from psychology. Developing a cycle theory of violence, which demonstrates that there are different periods within a violent couple's life which includes a period of love and kindness that binds one to the other, came from the empirical evidence. It came from looking through all of these stories.

In my research I have looked at battered women as victims of battering behavior, rather than exploring the causes of violence. Del Martin presents detailed evidence on how a sexist society facilitates a woman's battering. Police, courts, hospitals, social services, all refuse to provide them protection. Psychologists, too, have learned to keep the family together at all costs, even if the individual's mental health or life is at stake. Many of the battered women interviewed told of the psychiatric hospitalization and treatment for diagnoses that did not take into account their lives with violence. A transient, generalized stress reaction from constantly being abused is the most typical psychiatric label for battered women. If the physician did not have knowledge of the woman's abuse, the diagnoses were typically neurotic and psychotic rather than reactive.

Just as Eva Paterson tries to demystify some of the criminal justice system, I am going to try to demystify some of the psychological services system, because I think the mental health profession is also guilty of keeping people in this violent atmosphere. The interviews that I have conducted indicate that almost every one of the myths that mental health professionals associate with battered women are simply not true. Women *do not* like being beaten and they are *not* masochistic. They remain with their batterer because of economics, dependency, children, terror, fear, and often because they simply have no safe place to go. Their victimization often causes them compelling psychological problems, which then blind them into these kinds of symbiotic relationships. Too many psychologists prefer to diagnose and label women as mentally ill, particularly paranoid, rather than understand the survival behavior their symptoms represent. I am currently involved in a legal case in Denver, in which professionals have made this mistake because they did not have enough information about battered women's behavior to act differently. Eventually, both the men and the women of violence become frightened that they cannot survive alone. Thus, one of the most important tasks for anybody working with battered women is to restore their self-esteem and help them to learn that they can indeed survive alone. In fact, the more work I have done in this area, the more often I do not ask the question "Why didn't she leave?". Instead I ask the questions "What are the strengths within this woman that have permitted her to survive living in the kind of hell that she lives in? How is it she is not killed?" That is the question we need to look at and to study.

The Cycle of Battering: Three Phases

Rather than constant or random occurrences of battering, there is a definite cycle which is repeated over a period of time in long-term battering relationships. This cycle appears to have three distinct phases that vary with time and intensity, both within the same couple and between different couples. I have labeled these three phases descriptively. The first one is the tension-building phase; the second one is the explosion, or the acute battering incident; and the third one is the calm, loving, respite stage. So far it has been difficult to discern how long a couple will remain in any one phase or to predict the length of any one cycle. There is a lot of evidence that situational events can influence the timing. Relationships that have lasted 20 or more years indicate that there are different cycle patterns corresponding to the different stages of life. For example, one woman that I interviewed had lived with her batterer for 36 years. She reported that in the beginning of their relationship the beatings were not very frequent or very severe. Once they had children they became closer together and more brutal. She spent several weeks during her third pregnancy recuperating from a particularly violent bashing. As her childen were growing up, the beatings were not as devastating, nor did they occur as often as they had when the children were very little. Once the children became teen-agers, however, the beatings again became severe and remained so until the children left the household. When they left the home, there were no more acute battering incidents for a period of 10 years. Throughout all of this, psychological harassment and terror remained intense, but a physical explosion did not occur. This couple could have been characterized as being in a tension-building phase for that time, due to sufficient ways of coping and maintaining which prevented an explosion, until one of the children was killed in an unfortunate accident. At that time, the man handled his grief by beating the woman so seriously that when I met her she had been recuperating for three months in the hospital. Several years have passed since then without a repeated explosion. This means that we, as helpers, also have to be able to look at some of the natural ways people who live in a battering relationship can maintain status quo.

Phase 1

Let me tell a little bit more about the cycles and some of the different patterns in the phases. Phase 1, the tension-building phase, is described as one in which the tension begins to rise and the woman can sense that the man is becoming edgy and more prone to react negatively to any minor frustration. There can be minor episodes of violence, which are very quickly covered up. He may begin to lash out at her for some real or imagined wrongdoing and then quickly apologize and become docile again. Many women have learned to catch these outbursts and attempt to calm the batterer down by using techniques which have had previous success. She may become nurturing, compliant, and anticipate his every whim or she may just stay out of his way. She lets the batterer know, however, that she accepts the abusiveness as legitimately being directed toward her. She believes that if she does this, she will prevent his anger from escalating. If she does her job well, the incident will be over. If he explodes, she has then put herself in the position where she now accepts the guilt. If she had been better at keeping him calmer, which was the job she has now internalized, he would not have exploded. In order for her to maintain this no-win role, the battered woman must not permit herself to get angry with her batterer. She uses the psychological defense mechanism of denial: she denies her anger at being unfairly abused. She reasons that perhaps she did deserve the abuse and she often identifies with her aggressor's faulty reasoning. We see this when we work as helpers with battered women who tell us they are not angry and who seem to have a need not to be angry with their batterer, but rather internalize the anger against themselves. They were not good enough. This does work for a little while to postpone the inevitable second phase, and that is why it continues to be used. Women who have been battered over a period of time know that these minor incidents will get worse; however, they deny this knowledge in order to help themselves cope. They also deny the terror of the inevitable second phase by attempting to believe that they have some control over the batterer's behavior.

During the initial stages of this first phase, they do indeed have some limited control. As the tension builds they rapidly lose this control. *Each time* a minor battering incident occurs, there are residual tension-building effects. Her anger steadily increases, even though she does not recognize it or express it. He is aware of the inappropriateness of his behavior, even if he does not acknowledge it. He becomes more fearful that she may leave him and she reinforces this fear because she further withdraws from him to avoid inadvertently setting off an impending explosion. He becomes more oppressive, jealous, and possessive in the hope that his brutality and his threats will keep her captive, and often it does. As the batterer and the battered woman sense the escalating tension, it becomes more difficult for their coping mechanisms to continue working. Each becomes more frantic. The man increases his possessive smothering and brutality and psychological humiliation becomes more barbed. Battering incidents become more frequent and last longer. The battered woman is unable to restore equilibrium. She is less able to psychologically defend against the pain and hurt. The psychological torture is reported to be the worst and the women say it is far more serious to deal with than is the physical pain. To protect herself, she usually withdraws more from the batterer and then he moves more oppressively toward her until the point of inevitability is reached and the next phase, the acute battering incident, occurs.

Sometimes the battered woman cannot stand the tension any longer. She knows an explosion is inevitable but she does not know how or where it will occur. These women will often be at their wits' end and will provoke an incident. They do not do it to be hurt. They do it because they know they will be abused no matter what else they do, and they would prefer to get the incident over with on their own turf. Then they can be prepared to deal with it. Somehow these few women reason if they can name the time and place of the explosion, they will still have retained some control. They also know that once the acute explosion is over, the batterer will move into the third phase of calm, loving behavior. Thus, their reward is not the beating, as the masochistic myth would have it, but rather the kind, loving husband they will have after it is over.

Phase 2

During Phase 2, the batterer fully accepts the fact that his rage is out of control. In Phase 1 his violence is usually very carefully controlled: they are small incidents. In Phase 2, the batterer may start out by justifying his behavior to himself; however, it usually ends with him not understanding what has happened. In his blind rage, and it *is* blind rage at this point, he usually starts out wanting to teach her a lesson for some wrong-doing that he thinks she has committed. The batterers report that they do not start out wanting to hurt their woman, but they want to teach her a lesson and that is what they concentrate on. He only stops when he feels that he has taught her a lesson. What makes him stop we do not know; maybe he simply becomes exhausted. Batterers have a great deal of difficulty in talking about what happens during the acute phase. They seem out of control both physically and emotionally, thus not allowing them to record or recall the event and certainly not allowing them to give us any information about what causes them to stop.

The same is not true of the battered woman. She can tell in detail exactly who did what to whom during that period of time. It is as though she disassociates her mind from her body and she is like a fly on the wall observing what has happened. It is a wonderful psychological mechanism which helps her cope with the phenomenal amounts of pain she should be experiencing at the time. She does a lot of disassociating from any perception of pain and focuses on surviving the incident. Many women who have been damming up their anger during the

entire first phase feel safe letting out their anger during the
second phase. At times, women will report fighting back at this
point. However, they know they are going to be beaten anyway
and most women who do report fighting back also state that
they feel they are only battered worse during the incident.

Battered women describe incidents which have absolutely
no ground or reason. It is not uncommon for the batterer to
wake the woman from a deep sleep to begin his assault. Most
women are severely grateful when the battering ends. They
consider themselves lucky that it was not worse, no matter
how bad their injuries are. They often deny the seriousness
of their injuries and refuse to seek immediate medical attention. They do not permit themselves to feel the pain. Sometimes this is done to appease the batterer and make certain that
Phase 2 really is finished and not just temporarily halted.

Phase 2 is the most violent point of the cycle. It is also the
shortest. It seems to last somewhere between a few hours and
perhaps 24 to 48 hours. Generally, it is not reported as lasting
much longer than that, although in some cases it has. There
is a high incidence of police fatalities at this time. That is
because the police are intervening at a time when rage is
totally out of control. It is sheer madness to train police officers
to be social workers and go in to conciliate when rage is so out
of control. When a couple reaches this stage it is absolutely
necessary to separate the two people, and not for just a walk
around the block.

Phase 3

The ending of Phase 2 and movement into the third phase,
which is characterized by extremely loving, kind, contrite
behavior, is welcomed by both parties. It is during the third
phase of this cycle that the battered woman's victimization
becomes complete. Her man is genuinely sorry for what he has
done, even though he often does not tell her so overtly and
he tries with the same sense of overkill that is seen in the pre-

vious phases to make it up to her. His worst fear is that she will leave him and he is charming and manipulative enough to attempt to make sure that this does not happen. He believes that he can control himself and will never again hurt this woman whom he loves, and that is an important point that we must not forget. There is an enormous love bond between the couple that is set up during this phase. He manages to convince everybody concerned at this point that this time he means it. He will give up his drinking, dating other women, visiting his mother, reduce his workload, or whatever else affects his internal anxiety. His sincerity is believable. The battered woman wants to believe that she will no longer have to suffer abuse. His reasonableness and his loving behavior during this period supports her wish that he really can change. She convinces herself that he can do what he says he wants to do. It is during Phase 3 that the woman gets a glimpse of her original dream of how wonderful love is although it is based on romanticism rather than mature kinds of loving behavior— this is a phase of idealization.

I first realized how idealized this phase was when I was being called to the hospital to visit some women who were hospitalized immediately following their beatings. The first day that I would walk in to interview these women following the beating, they would be very angry and would be able to tell me detail for detail exactly what happened. Right after the crisis their anger and fury is at its height. Once somebody asked me if I would come back the next day. I came back the second day and this woman who had been lying there kind of small and frail the first time that I was there was already much more perky on the second day. She had combed her hair a little bit, even though she had very severe injuries. But what was the most noticeable were the flowers all over the room. By the third day the flowers were not only all over her room, but they spilled out into the nurses' station in the corridor. There were flowers and candy everywhere. I could not believe what I was seeing. Along with these flowers, the woman's story started to soften. I had already gotten the details from her the first time around. By the second and the third day she was not so angry with him because he had been working on her. He called her every 10 or 15 minutes while I was sitting in the room. Not only did he call her but he also enlisted the support of everybody who had ever liked him at any time in his life to call her. "You cannot leave," they told her. "You absolutely can't. He will fall apart without you." You know something, they were absolutely right. He would fall apart without her and she knew it. Now, not only is she responsible for her own victimization and her own beating she is also responsible if this guy falls apart because she pulled out. She cannot win.

Battered women are very much adored during this third phase. They are given everything they want, and the clue to watch for is the sense of overkill. One woman told me she had a favorite perfume and she wanted a little bottle, one-quarter of an ounce, yet he bought her a four-ounce bottle. Another woman said to me, "I really used to think it was great, all these gifts and presents, and things that I would get during this phase, but the last one was a Cadillac and I can't afford to pay for it, and I'm still making the payments on it." She was still being assaulted but this time with all of his wonderful gifts.

The time that this third phase lasts is not known yet either. There just has not been enough work done. It seems to be longer than the second phase, but shorter than the first phase. The tension-building phase tends to be the longest phase in the cycle. In some cases, Phase 3 is so short it almost defies detection. However, it exists in most of the cases I have looked at and others that have been reported. Before one knows it, the tension starts to build again; there is another little incident here and another little one there and the cycle begins over again.

Understanding the cycle theory is important. It is important because once it is recognized, we can teach it to men and women. We can teach women not to fall for the charming, wonderful, loving man in their batterer, but understand that he really has the split personality they define. What happens is that battered women say their men are either charming and very loving or they are very mean and very horrible. The reality of their dual personality needs to be reaffirmed. What women want to believe is that somehow if they can do something better or somebody else can fix it all up, magically the bad part of him will totally disappear and the good part of him will win out. Now, truthfully, that does not happen. What happens in the cases that I have followed over a long period of time is just the opposite. The good part of him tends to get smaller and smaller and the meanness tends to take over.

In the cases in which I have testified as an expert witness for women who have killed their batterers in self-defense, it was at the point that this bad part of the man started taking over and the men themselves had told the women "you had better kill me because I'm just out of control" and it was generally an instantaneous choice of whether he was going to kill her or she was going to kill him. In a few cases that I have been involved in when the woman killed him, she states that she only wanted to stop him from inflicting further harm to her. She usually does not realize he is dead until later. I do not know how many men have killed the woman before this point is reached. Reading the daily newspaper makes me suspect it is more frequent than previously imagined.

The lethality of this cycle we are talking about must not be ignored as we attempt to intervene in it. The possibility of dying is a strong component in battering relationships. I am convinced that the sense of death is different for people who have lived a long time in violence than it is for those who have not. There is some sense of welcome relief as well as non-permanence about death to those who have learned to live with violence. Battered women whose husbands or batterers have died still believe, months and sometimes years afterward, that the man still has control over them. They feel as though he still has the power to watch and regulate their behavior.

Breaking The Cycle

What can we do? It is far easier to be taken in by this seductive, manipulative behavior when one does not know what is happening, than when one does. Education is far and wide the best tool that we have. It is important to educate people so they understand what happens in these cycles and how to break them. It helps to conceptualize ways of breaking this cycle if we use a public health model. This acknowledges that there is a malady which is causing an epidemiological problem. Domestic violence is not due to a pathological disease of a few and I cannot stress that enough. Rather, it is a psychosocial disorder of society at large. There are no easy medicines to prescribe; rather, we need a systematic approach that affects every level of society so we can slowly eliminate this problem through long-term social change while at the same time we must provide support for those women who are presently being wounded. Preventive approaches will eventually be the only way to eliminate domestic violence on a long-term level.

Let us look at some intermediate steps: first of all, the safe house or shelter movement and, secondly, some psychotherapeutic techniques. The safe house, refuge, or shelter has been the cornerstone for helping battered women break the bonding between themselves and their batterer and rebuild their lives.

Shelters

It began in England in 1971 when Erin Pizzey founded Chiswick Woman's Aid and it has grown so fast in that country that there are over 120 refuges open. Think of it: England is the size of Pennsylvania and they have 120 refuges already. We do not have that many in this entire country. However, it has clearly been a goal of most battered women's groups to have a shelter open to serve every community. This goal makes good sense, even though a shelter is not a panacea and will never service the needs of all women. If my estimate that one out of two women will experience violence at some time is anywhere near accurate, shelters cannot begin to fill the needs. Why do I think it is so important then? First of all, they provide immediate safety for a battered woman and her children, which is something no other agency or institution has ever done in this society. This is essential during Phase 2 of the battering cycle. It is essential to help people recognize the impending Phase 2 explosion so they come to shelters *before* the acute battering incident. Reports are that more women are starting to do that as we have more publicity, which has probably been the best thing that could happen for battered women. The more the media report it, the more conferences we have, the more people talk about it, the more battered women will stand up and say, "No more. I'm not going to stand for it anymore." No other intervention technique besides separating those two people will be of use during that second phase. It also prevents the third phase from happening because the shelter protects the woman from the man's showering all those flowers and candy and phone calls and other sources of love on her. She cannot be intimidated at that point because she is safely hidden from him during the immediate crisis period. The cycle is at least broken for a short time at that point. Furthermore, the existence of a shelter in a community stands out as a commitment by the community that it will not tolerate assault. It will not tolerate a man beating a woman. If he assaults her anyway, he faces the possible consequences of losing her. It dissuades many batterers from beating their women.

Just the existence of a shelter should influence the tension-building phase from escalating further, so it does serve as a deterrent to those whom it may never serve. The other thing that a shelter does is force other community institutions to start dealing with the problem. I do not advocate a separatist system of dealing with battered women. I do not believe that either the feminist movement or those of us committed to eliminating the problem have the resources or the wherewithal to be able to do it. We must force all of our existing institutions to start doing what they are trained to do, and that is to assist people who need some kind of services. A shelter can do it, but it can only do it if it works with other community people. That means some compromise and there are all kinds of ideological problems about doing that. Most serious is the fear of being co-opted in order to gain support from other professionals in the community. If there is no support from community mental health centers, police departments, social service agencies, and all the other community helpers we have set up in this country, battered women will not receive adequate services. They need all of those services, in addition to a place to be safe for a while.

Psychotherapy

Let us look at some of the kinds of psychotherapy that would be useful in working with battered women. First of all, I feel the only therapy of choice at the moment is feminist-oriented psychotherapy. Remember, battered women tend to be women who believe the traditional dream, they do not tend to be feminist while they are being battered. Although feminists find themselves being battered, they tend not to remain in a battering relationship for a long period of time. That is how I first learned of the problem. It was the feminist women who were coming to me and talking about it in outraged tones. The women we are talking about, who are most likely to need feminist therapy related to issues of battering, are traditional women.

Feminist therapy does not mean that we are making feminists out of traditional women. This is something which has been very difficult to explain to people. What feminist therapy means is that the therapist is prowoman, someone who really believes in the strength of being a woman and who spends her time in helping the woman separate her own personal, psychological issues which are getting in her way from the issues which are common to all women living in this society. What they are doing is taking that first phase of the battering cycle and helping the woman understand what she does, what *is* her problem, what may be provocative, and what is not her fault at all, but is being contributed to her by both her batterer and by society. Feminist therapy also includes advocacy for a client, not a neutral stance. All possible choices and options are explored. It includes making the therapist's values very explicit. I say "her" advisedly, because at this stage of the game, I think the feminist therapist must be a woman. My colleagues do not always agree with me, especially the male psychology professionals, but I believe that. Battered women have learned to relate to men in a very charming, seductive way. That is the way they have learned, that is why they are in the bind they are in at this time. If the therapist is male, there is a lot of extra time spent learning how to relate to a man in a different kind of way when the most critical issue is learning how to survive at that moment, learning how to stop being battered. She has time for long-term work on improving her relationships with men later on. The first thing she has to learn is how to gain some safety for herself and regain some of her self-esteem. Therapy takes longer when the therapist is male, although it can be successful and I have seen some very profeminist men who do well.

I do not advocate couples therapy. It does not cure violence. All it does is reduce the severity and frequency with which violent episodes occur. What we do is keep them in the first tension-building phase of the cycle for a longer period of time and then we teach them communication skills. We teach them not to let their anger build up. One of the imperatives between men and women who are involved in this kind of violence is that neither one of them wants confrontation. They fear anger, and they cannot deal with it so they avoid the little angry confrontations that we have on a day-to-day basis. They build it up and store it until there is an explosion. It seems to be a contradiction, but it makes psychological sense.

Group therapy techniques have been the most successful for both men and women. For men it is early, we are just starting to get men into treatment. You need a carrot to get a man into psychotherapy treatment. The carrot is the woman. What a battered women should do is suggest that maybe if he is willing to come into treatment, she might consider living together again.

The critical element here is to break that symbiotic bond. What we are dealing with are not two independent human beings. We are dealing with a relationship in which the two people believe they can only survive if they are together. What we have to do in psychotherapy is teach each one of them to be independent people, then they may be able to make an interdependent relationship. Until each one of them feels whole and able to stand on his and her own, they will not be able to do it. I disagree with the marital therapists who say that we must treat the relationship. I want to treat the individuals within the relationship so they can change the nature of the relationship to a healthy interaction between two healthy people.

The shelters for battered women are utilizing crisis intervention techniques. They must work with women when they first come in after leaving their men. Some shelters are now starting to deal with the men in crisis, too. Some of these women have been damaged over a long period of living in violence; they need psychotherapy or some other method with which they can regain some of their self-esteem. After they have a healthy level of self-esteem, the kind of therapy they need is not the kind that explores all of their reasons for why they did what they did. A battered woman does not have time to be analyzed, nor does she have time to go into all kinds of self-analysis. What she needs is some behavioral, action-oriented techniques on a short-term basis.

Let me conclude by saying that community mental health centers could and should be providing these therapeutic services. Not everyone, however, is trained or suited to be a therapist to men, women, or children of violence. Selection of the best person to give therapy when therapy is indicated is still an imperfect process.

There are, however, some attitudes and values one might look for in selecting a therapist for people who have been living in violence. I will briefly list these qualities I feel we in the mental health profession must possess to effectively work with battered women.

The first thing is an attitude of support for women who have been victimized. We must understand that it is the battered woman who is the victim, not the perpetrator. The second attitude is one that does not accept stereotypic myths about battering relationships which are false. A therapist must appreciate natural support systems within a community and also be willing to help create new support systems. Therapists must cooperate and untangle bureaucracy for unskilled clients. We must collaborate with other professionals, even if we do not like their politics. We must deal with our own fear of violence, and most of us have fears. We also have to understand how institutions oppress and reinforce the victimization of women. We must be willing to be a role model for our clients. We must be willing to work with messy and complicated cases. We must appreciate the work of noncredentialed paraprofessionals. We must be able to formulate outlets for our own anger. We must tolerate clients' anger. We also must tolerate horror stories and terrorizing events. We have to allow our clients to work through their own issues without pushing them too fast, even though we are scared to death that they are going to die. We must also allow our clients to return to violent relationships without becoming angry with them. We must have respect and belief in people's capacity to change and to grow and we also must be a woman or a person who holds feminist values.

Suggested Readings

Davidson, T. *Conjugal Crime* (New York: Hawthorne Books, 1978).

Walker, L. E. Treatment alternatives for battered women. In J. R. Chapman & M. Gates (eds.) *The victimization of women* (Beverly Hills: Sage, 1978).

Walker, L. E. "Battered women and learned helplessness." *Victimology: An International Journal*, Vol. 2 February 1978.

HOW THE LEGAL SYSTEM RESPONDS TO BATTERED WOMEN

Eva Jefferson Paterson

Introduction

Historical Views About Battered Women

The purpose of this chapter is to give an overview of both how the legal system does and does not respond to battered women. I would also like to present a series of concrete proposals for how to change the legal system to make it more responsive, protective, and supportive of the needs of battered women.

First, I want to look at how the law does not protect battered women. Historically, the law has viewed women as property or as children. Women were not allowed to make contracts because they were put in the same category as idiots and incompetents. The rationale was that women did not have the intellectual capacity to make the kinds of decisions that men could make. So the law, in a view that was seen as protective at the time, stopped women from exercising all their rights and from acting as full and competent people in society.

One of the ways the law worked for women was in trying to

protect them from being beaten too severely. The way women were protected was very bizarre indeed. The thought was that women should not be beaten too severely and there should be some way of protecting them from the violence of men, so the "rule of thumb" was developed which was put into effect in the last century. The rule of thumb said that a man could beat his wife as long as the stick he used was no thicker than his thumb. The bottom line was that women were not equals and were unable to act as whole people in society. The law gave credence to the idea that women are allowed to be beaten; that women are property; that women belong to their husbands. Since women are like children, they should be disciplined like children; a slap on the face or a thrashing with a good sturdy stick was an acceptable and legal way to keep them in line. The law was, and is, merely a reflector of societal attitudes and must be understood within that context. The rule of thumb articulates a nonresponsive societal attitude toward women which has been institutionalized by the nonresponsiveness of the courts, the district attorneys, the police, the attorneys, and the whole continuum of the criminal justice system.

Criminal Justice System as a Reflection of Societal Attitudes

The criminal justice system in its general nonresponsiveness to the plight of battered women merely reflects the views held in the society at large. For centuries, beating women has been the norm for societies around the world and has rarely been viewed as criminal activity. In fact, husbands were given free rein by the legal system to discipline their wives through the use of physical violence.

The criminal justice system usually reflects societal attitudes. Since the society at large did not feel criminal sanctions should be imposed for wife beating, law enforcement officials did not feel they had to enforce the criminal laws in this area. This is a phenomenon which is common in history and one which is not peculiar to battering. For example, societal attitudes about rape have undergone a dramatic change in the past few years primarily because of the work of feminists. These attitudes are now being reflected by the criminal justice system: police are actively investigating and arresting suspects in rape cases; district attorneys are taking rape cases to court and winning; judges are imposing harsh sentences for men convicted of rape. It is important that society give the criminal justice system the same type of clear message that battering women is not acceptable in order that it might begin changing the manner in which it deals with the plight of battered women.

The Oakland and New York Lawsuits

Many women who have been the victims of domestic violence have called various police departments for assistance. In many cases, the police have not been particularly helpful to these women. The police either have not come to the home of the woman or, if they have, they have not seen the beatings as crimes and have therefore not taken any action which might help correct the situation. Many of these women went to legal aid offices and complained about the nonresponsiveness of the police departments. Attorneys in New York and Oakland examined the situation and determined that the women in these cities were not being afforded the full protection of the laws and of the police. As a result, class action lawsuits were brought against the police departments of Oakland and New York charging that the police had violated various rights of the women. As of July 1978, both police departments had lost motions in court to dismiss the actions and have agreed to make basic changes in departmental policy regarding handling domestic violence situations. In both cities the police are going to increase their intervention in these cases and will make arrests of the batterers using the same criteria used in other assault cases. These are only two examples of how societal attitudes have been effective in changing the way the criminal justice system responds to battered women.

Legal Problems in Working With Battered Women

Civil versus Criminal Charges:
The Need To See This as a Crime

Although in many instances the injuries suffered by battered women can be the basis for civil damage actions, there is a danger in viewing domestic violence as solely or primarily a civil problem. In a civil suit against the batterer, the injured woman usually recovers only money damages. In addition to a damage recovery, she can also obtain an order from the court ordering her assailant to cease and desist from further abusive behavior. Since the only enforcer of such an order is the police, a woman is in trouble if her local police department has a policy of nonresponse to calls from women who have temporary restraining orders whose terms are being violated. Thus, if the police continue to view domestic violence as a civil matter, the civil remedies available to the woman (such as obtaining a temporary restraining order) will remain ineffective and the woman will be unprotected.

Police departments across the country have typically viewed domestic violence as a social problem and not as criminal conduct. Consequently, when women who have been battered call the police for assistance, they rarely receive the type of help normally associated with police intervention—namely, the arrest of the assailant if probable cause for such an arrest exists. Police officials have adopted the attitude that women who have been battered should be referred to social service agencies and actively counsel their officers to avoid arrests in domestic violence situations. The primary model for dealing with these problems is the dispute intervention model which calls for officers involved in domestic violence incidents to try to cool the parties down and not to take sides. This is a rather curious approach to assaults—an approach which has proven to do a disservice to battered women across the country. Men are getting the message from police officers that woman battering is not a crime and that the sanctions of the criminal justice system—sanctions which presumably exist to deter and punish those who have the inclination to behave in antisocial ways—are routinely not invoked by police officers and that therefore they have nothing to fear if they beat the women with whom they are, or were, involved. Now that attitudes are undergoing a transformation in this whole area, law enforcement officials should change their policies accordingly and provide battered women the protection they so desperately need.

Temporary Restraining Orders: Their Effectiveness, When the Police Department Can/Cannot Use Them

The legal system is beginning to change the manner in which it protects women from the assaults of abusive men. Women's groups in California lobbied the legislature regarding the failure of the criminal justice system to adequately protect women and achieved the passage of legislation aimed at providing increased protection for women. One of these pieces of legislation broadens the scope of temporary restraining orders which women can obtain to protect themselves from abusive men. The law used to grant restraining orders only to women who were in the process of dissolving their marriages. If a woman was unable or unwilling to get a divorce from her husband or if the woman was merely living with the alleged assailant, she could not obtain a restraining order. The law has been changed to allow any person, man or woman, to obtain a temporary restraining order which orders the cessation of any violence perpetrated by a member of the opposite sex. Police departments are beginning to change their policies on enforcement of temporary restraining orders in domestic violence cases and are starting to treat the violation of a restraining order as an offense which merits police intervention. Toward that end, many police departments are developing new methods of responding to calls from women who feel the men they are involved with or were involved with are violating the terms of a temporary restraining order. Consequently, women will have a much easier time obtaining protection from abusive men.

One legal problem is that the police are not allowed to make an arrest unless a felony has been committed or unless a misdemeanor has been committed in their presence. The police have a way of seeing assaults against women as misdemeanors and that way they can say they have not witnessed the assault, therefore they cannot arrest. If a man violates a temporary restraining order which says that he is not supposed to be in Mary Jones's house, that is a misdemeanor committed in the presence of the police officer who arrives at her home and finds the man there. Police officers then have the right to make an arrest, but they generally do not. We need to educate police officers regarding their ability to make such misdemeanor arrests for violations of temporary restraining orders and further educate women so they know what they can legally insist that a police officer do regarding her temporary restraining order.

Why The Police Do Not Act

The police argue that the district attorneys do not charge and the judges do not sentence batterers, so the police department should not waste its time making such arrests. Remember that for a police officer, the reward is in making arrests which result in convictions. So if the district attorney or the judge is not taking the crime seriously, the police officer is going to quit making arrests. As one can see, it is not just the police, it is the entire criminal justice system which fails the battered woman. Why is the system unresponsive? Battering is not seen as a crime. Many people in this society see battering as a legitimate means of dealing with relationship problems. Studies have shown that the more educated one is, the more acceptable one perceives wife beating to be, and as I have said above, the criminal justice system simply reflects societal attitudes.

A strange attitude exhibited by the police is an unexplainable and unusual concern for the rights of the accused, which is rarely manifested in other types of crimes. The police make statements such as "He can't make bail," or "He's going to lose face," all of which one can say for any other crime, but they particularly use these excuses in battering situations.

Police also say "Well the women are hysterical. They are screaming and crying and how can we deal with them? We can't help them." Well, if I got hit in the face, I think I might be crying too. I do not think it is an inappropriate response to be emotionally upset if you have just been beaten up. So a third reason the police may not respond is that they have not been trained to handle emotions typically expressed by battered women, so they would rather ignore the obvious problem. Remember that it has not been too many years since women's groups have helped police departments to respond appropriately to the emotions displayed by sexual assault victims. Police officers have learned to handle sexual assault victims and there is no reason to believe, given some assistance, that they could not learn to respond equally well to battered women.

Another major reason police do not like to respond to domestic violence calls is that they are the single most risky call for police officers. More police officers are killed, and injured, answering these calls than in any other kind of crime. But one must remember that women are killed while being battered. Responding to these calls is dangerous, but police officers have their lives on the line all the time; it goes with the territory. We hire police because we want them to take those kinds of risks to protect us. We want them to physically protect us. I would not want to walk into a situation in which the chances of my getting killed were greater than some other type of crime. On the other hand, inaction means women are being brutalized and often killed.

Why Charges Are Dropped

One of the primary reasons given by members of the criminal justice system for nonresponsiveness to the plight of battered women is the fact that women who have been battered and who call the police for assistance often decide to drop the charges. Although there are many reasons for this phenomenon, it does justifiably frustrate members of the criminal justice system. Many women change their minds about pressing charges against their assailants because they do not want to see the men they are involved with imprisoned or because the assailant has threatened further violence if the woman pursues the complaint. If society were able to provide support for these women, perhaps they might be able to withstand the pressure. Alameda County, California, has a fine victim assistance program which gives women emotional support when they are faced with having to press charges against assailants. Perhaps if other localities adopted a similar program, fewer women would feel compelled to drop charges. Another means of support which has proven to be most effective has been the establishment of shelters for battered women. Such shelters are helpful for several reasons. They give women the physical and psychological space to carefully evaluate the relationships they were involved in and to determine whether there is any merit in the continuation of these relationships. Women who are battered are often very isolated and do not realize that other women have found themselves in similar situations. Being around other battered women helps end the sense of isolation. Often these women realize for the very first time that they may not be entirely responsible for the violence which has been inflicted upon them. Through communication with other women, those who have been battered can often increase their sense of self-worth and begin to build new lives either with or without the batterers.

Now that we have taken a brief look at historical views of battering and legal problems in working with battered women, let us look at how the three major arms of the criminal justice system respond to battered women.

Police Departments

Responses to Battered Women

Let us look at what happens when a woman calls the police. First of all, in many cases no one responds to the call. The woman sits and waits and no one shows up. This seems to be a particularly cruel response to women. If a woman feels that the police are going to help her and then nobody responds, that is a horrible situation. Imagine being in a position in which you have called the police and are desperate for help and they never arrive.

Another possibility is that the police respond, but they side with the batterer. There is a companion case to the lawsuit brought against the Oakland Police that has been brought in New York called *Bruno v. Codd.* In this case, a police officer came into a situation in which a woman had been brutally beaten and the police officer looked at the batterer and said, "Well, maybe if I slap my wife around a couple of times she might behave too." Now this is after a woman has called— desperate for help—and the police officer comes in and sides with the batterer. What I am describing is the worst of all possible worlds. There are police departments which are responsive, just as there are police officers who care about battered women, but in any article on battered women there is always a section which describes police inaction. No matter how one feels about this issue, nonresponsiveness is a common denominator running through experiences of battered women with the police. I do not want to alienate sympathetic police officers, but I also do not want to sell out the interest of battered women by pretending that the police always help, because in many cases they do not.

The third classic response of the police officer is to say, "Listen buddy, take a walk around the block, cool down, get a grip on yourself." Then the police leave and what happens is that the man comes back and is even more enraged because "his" woman has had the audacity to publicize his abuse of her. At this point he is more angry and the police are gone, so she is going to get more physical and emotional abuse.

A fourth response of the police occurs in the situation in which the woman is separated from the man or they might be just seeing each other and not living together. The man comes in, slaps her around, and then leaves. The woman wants the man apprehended but when the police arrive they say they do not have time to do that, they are too busy. Women feel they do not have any help in this particular instance. My response has been that when Patty Hearst or the Symbionese Liberation Army left the scene the police never said, "Well, it's a little too much trouble to find them, maybe they'll turn up later." Obviously that is an extreme example, but I think the reader gets my point.

Another typical response which highlights the fact that this particular offense is often not seen as a crime is the view that all domestic violence is a civil matter. Police officers who take this position often tell battered women to talk to their lawyers and get a temporary restraining order. Since temporary restraining orders are not enforced, this advice is like the Wizard of Oz telling Dorothy to get the witch's red shoes. The officer knows it is not going to do any good, but it is a way of buying some time. The police are as frustrated with the situation as the rest of us so they characterize the matter as a civil matter and do not deal with it.

If one already has a temporary restraining order, police come and say "How do we know the temporary restraining order is still in effect? This is just a piece of paper." The Oakland, California Police Department had a policy of *not* enforcing temporary restraining orders which has been changed as the result of effective litigation. Police officers often say it is a civil matter and one must go to the district attorney, but the infuriating part of all this is that the whole purpose of the restraining orders is to allow the police to respond and take the man away. The police are the very people who are supposed to enforce these orders but, as we discussed earlier, they are not doing so and need some eduation and encouragement to use their ability to arrest a man who is in violation of a temporary restraining order.

In a situation in which the woman wants the man removed, the police sometimes say, "Well, his clothes are here, he's here, and you two look like you live together. How can I throw him out? He has equal right to the property." They assume that the man has the right to be there. It might be helpful for them to take a look at the lease to see whose name is on it. I understand this is a very volatile situation and police officers cannot leaf through legal papers but it might be valuable to find out who is paying the rent—maybe the man does not have any legal right to be there. The police should not make the automatic assumption that the man has a right to be in the home or that he has equal rights with the woman to be there, because that is not necessarily true. The police often say this is a civil matter and suggest that the woman go to the district attorney, swear out a complaint, and get a warrant. The problem with this is that it is often 3 a.m. Saturday and the man is standing there beating her up. She does not have time to walk down to the district attorney's office and swear out a complaint. She also may not live until Monday morning when the district attorney's office opens up.

This problem is difficult for lawyers, district attorneys, police, and the entire criminal justice system. We cannot just turn our backs on battered women because many women are being killed: women are being hurt physically and psychologically. We cannot look away just because this is a difficult problem.

Another way police officers often respond is to discourage the woman from making a citizen's arrest when she has the right to do so. If you hit me and I want to make a citizen's arrest, it is a felony for the police officer not to make such an arrest. Yet, the police officers either do not tell the woman she has the right to make such an arrest, or they discourage her from doing so, or they simply refuse to make the arrest. The police say, "Look, you really don't want to arrest him do you? He's going to have to use the rent money to make bail and you really don't want to do that." The police say the justification for this is that arresting someone inconveniences the family and is embarrassing. I have never heard of somebody not being arrested after robbing a grocery store because it would be embarrassing to arrest them or they could have trouble making bail. Or how about if you kill someone and the police say they will not embarrass you by arresting you or putting you in jail because you probably could not make bail. Do you see the point? In this particular type of situation the police make excuses for not seeing it as a crime. Excuses that would be laughable in any other situation. Yet because of the way society views domestic violence, it is seen as a valid way of perceiving the problem and of not reacting.

This goes much deeper than the whole battered women's issue. It goes to the whole idea of feminism: the whole idea that women have not been allowed to be strong and have not been able to control their own lives. If we tell a woman she has the right to make a citizen's arrest, but we are not going to do anything about it, that perpetuates the whole sense of powerlessness that women have. That is part of the root of this whole problem. The criminal justice system has got to stop doing everything it can to frustrate women from insisting on being protected.

Another way to avoid taking people into custody is to release them on a misdemeanor citation. A citation is issued when the police make a technical arrest but do not take the accused into custody; rather, they tell him to appear at the district attorney's office in three weeks or some future date to talk about the problem. This usually amounts to a slap on the hand, because nothing is likely to happen. One item that is in the misdemeanor citation law which the police often ignore is that if there is the possibility that violence is going to recur or if the assailant has a history of violence, the police are not supposed to release alleged batterers. This is something the police often do not seem to take into account in dealing with battering. They use this citation as a means of avoiding arrest.

It seems that the common denominator in this whole situation is that the police do not want to deal with batterers. They must stop this type of reaction. Batterings are going on and the police and their inaction are part of the problem. Once again, when the police fail to act, they are symbolically saying to people that it is all right to beat women and one does not have to worry about police intervention. One example I often use is that of the woman who got me involved in this whole issue initially, who was a battered woman herself. When her husband would start beating her he would hand her the telephone and say "Here, call the police." This portrays very graphically how batterers perceive what the police are going to do. Batterers feel like, "Hey, it's open season on women. I don't have anything to fear. The police aren't going to bother me. I might have to take a walk around the block and wait for the police to leave but then I can smack her all the more when I come back."

Needed Changes in Responding to Battered Women

We would like the police, the district attorneys, the judges, and everyone in the criminal justice system to have the attitude that beating up women is a crime. It is not something one looks away from. It is not a civil matter. It is a crime.

Most police manuals urge giving the highest priority to life-threatening situations. They do not seem to give the high priority they should to this particular life-threatening situation because they do not see it that way. Their perception is that it is just a little slap on the face. They do not understand, believe, or choose to see the criminal nature of these assaults. We want police officers to give wife battering the high priority they give other types of violent crimes.

We also do not want the police to always see battering as a misdemeanor. There is a felony wife-beating statute on the books in California and in many other states. It says that traumatic bodily injury inflicted on a woman by her husband is a felony. Batterers become very sophisticated. They hit women in the head, around the breasts, on the back, or upper legs— places where the bruises would not necessarily show. Pregnant women's stomachs are a particularly vulnerable target. In many cases police officers will not be able to see cuts or gashes. Bruises may not appear for a day or two. Just because a woman is not visibly bruised or bleeding the police officer must not assume that she has not been beaten. The police officer must take the woman seriously, listen to her, and help her.

We think there should be a whole new process of training police officers—or retraining them. The Oakland Police Department's training bulletin says a man will lose face if arrested for battering so he should not be arrested. This attitude is a disservice to battered women. We would like the police to be resensitized and retrained; we would like dispatchers to be sensitized because they are the people who have the first contact with women. We want them to be supportive and provide the assistance women need. We do not want them to tell women that a police officer will be at her home in five minutes when they know they are not even going to send anyone.

I think the police are not as aware of what is going on as most women are. Women have schooled themselves on this whole issue. Women have become familiar with the facts, the philosophy, and the psychology behind battering. The police need more of this type of information. Perhaps training by people from shelters, stories from battered women which let police officers know what a life of terror battered women live, and explanations of why women stay in this situation may help. The police need to understand.

Police officers must start telling women they have a right to make a citizen's arrest. In the New York lawsuit there is a list of the things the police must tell women when they go into homes. They should tell women they have a right to make a citizen's arrest and, more importantly, they should effectuate that arrest. They should take the man into custody. We think the police should not abuse this misdemeanor citation process. They should ask about violence in the background of the person. They should see if letting this man go is going to get the woman beaten up more. They should investigate more thoroughly what is going on and quit using the misdemeanor citation policy as an easy way out. They should not assume that temporary restraining orders are not valid. Putting temporary restraining orders into computers, similar to the way police departments handle traffic tickets, should be explored so police officers cannot say it is just a piece of paper but can quickly check to see if it is still in effect and should be enforced. The police must take temporary restraining orders seriously. The new temporary restraining order statute in California is very helpful although we have heard that some police departments have no intention of enforcing it.

There should be resource cards handed to women with the entire range of options they can consider in the situation. There is money available for such ideas and a resource card might be very helpful for women so they know what their options are, where to go to enact each option, and not feel quite so isolated.

District Attorneys

Responses to Battered Women

The Assault Detail of the Oakland Police Department is where the police send women when they say "Go down to the police and swear out a warrant. Then we can help you." Through depositions we learned that this Assault Detail actively discourages women from following through. They say, "Look, the District Attorney is not going to charge." They have a whole number of excuses and rationales they give to women for why they are not going to help. District attorneys often give the same excuses for nonaction that the police give: (1) domestic violence is not seen as a crime and is viewed as a purely personal matter involving only the batterer and the battered; (2) district attorneys have often been involved in instances of domestic violence in which the woman refused to follow through on the prosecution because of reconsideration of the consequences of a criminal prosecution or because of intimidating tactics practiced by the batterer; and (3) the district attorneys often feel they will not get a conviction from the judge.

At every phase of the criminal justice system, women are frustrated. If a woman who is being battered is not given support, she is not going to follow through. She is going to feel that society is not supporting her and that there is nothing she can do but accept the situation. That is something which must be changed.

Needed Changes in Responding to Battered Women

We have got to start talking to the district attorneys and asking why they are not charging and vigorously pursuing these cases. We need to convince them they are part of the problem. I understand the Los Angeles City Attorney's Office has set up a special Domestic Violence Unit to process these crimes. If there are vice squads, why cannot there be domestic violence squads? Battering is estimated to be the most frequently occuring crime in the country, so why can we not have a special unit that roots out this evil in our society and tries to deal with it? In addition, it might be helpful to reeducate district attorneys on the plight of battered women in an effort to get them to be more responsive and effective in dealing with these problems.

Judges

Information provided by both attorneys and battered women indicates that in the rare instance in which a batterer is

charged, judges are loathe to sentence these men for many of
the same reasons that police and district attorneys refuse to
act. We need to educate judges in the same way as we educate
police officers and district attorneys regarding the plight of
battered women. Further, we need to help judges think about
creative ways of sentencing batterers which might effectively
change their battering behaviors.

There is a judge in New Orleans who is apparently very
innovative in dealing with domestic violence. Once a person
has been brought before him, if all the facts are there and it
looks as if the person has battered the woman, he hands down a
sentence and then suspends it. The judge says "I'm going to
suspend this sentence, but if your wife comes in here one more
time and says that you have slapped her, you are going to jail."
This is one creative use of the criminal justice system which is
characterized as the carrot-and-stick approach. On the one
hand one could use the sanctions of the criminal justice system,
but on the other hand one could be hardhearted, coldblooded,
calculating, and inhumane about it. This interim approach
allows some toughness, but also gives people a break. There is
no clear-cut answer but I think we have to start talking about it
and get the issues out and start experimenting with some
changes so we can use the criminal justice system to protect
women. On the other hand, we do not want to just lock every
batterer up because ultimately that will not change either
battering behavior or societal attitudes.

Overview: Needed Changes in the Criminal Justice
System's Response to Battered Women

Despite the fact that much of this discussion has focused on
the role of the police in dealing with the problems battered
women face, the police are not solely responsible for the failure
of the criminal justice system to adequately respond to cries
for help. Because woman beating has been tolerated for so long
in our society, the criminal justice system has rarely been
willing to use its sometimes powerful sanctions to help mini-

mize this antisocial behavior. Now that societal attitudes are being transformed with regard to battering, attorneys, judges, and district attorneys must begin to change their behaviors and attitudes in an effort to be more supportive of battered women.

Many attorneys refuse to get involved in "domestic beefs." The rationale for this is usually that these matters are too time consuming and emotionally draining. Attorneys must change this attitude. They must assist women in obtaining temporary restraining orders. They must help them obtain protection if these restraining orders are violated. They must serve as counselors in an effort to rebuild and establish the self-esteem of the women. Attorneys must let women know that they are willing to assist in the civil and criminal prosecution of batterers.

Similarly, district attorneys must make or renew their commitments to prosecuting batterers. Police officers have often remarked that one of the reasons that they are hesitant to make arrests in domestic violence cases is that district attorneys do not take these offenses seriously and do not vigorously prosecute the alleged offenders. If this charge is correct, district attorneys must change this nonprotection policy. Judges also have been accused of refusing to see woman battering as a crime. It is imperative that this judicial attitude change so that a person who has brutally beaten a woman in a domestic situation is treated no differently than the mugger who brutally beats a citizen on the street.

One way of dealing with changing the attitudes and procedures of the criminal justice system is to have roundtable discussions which would include representatives of the police, the lawyers, the district attorney's office, the judiciary, and the battered women's movement. All the participants could discuss how they could and should change so that the criminal justice system can be truly responsive to the needs of battered women.

Despite the fact that this chapter has primarily stressed the inadequacies of the criminal justice system, many police departments, district attorneys, judges, and attorneys have begun to make changes in the way in which they deal with battered women. This action is commendable and should serve as a model for others who have not been so willing or able to change.

Conclusions

Ways to Make Changes Happen

If we work day and night for the next 80 years, there are still going to be men who beat up women. We have got to know that we are not going to eradicate the problem but that we can help. What I am saying is that we should not assume we are going to be able to change everybody, because that is unrealistic. The last thing I want to deal with is how to go about getting changes to happen in our society.

One very effective way to bring about change is through local politicking. It is going to be a struggle. It is not necessarily an unpleasant struggle but these attitudes and laws are not going to be changed immediately. Be ready to dig in and stick around for a while.

Another particularly good way to deal with change is through legislation. There is a group called the California Coalition Against Domestic Violence which did a lot of lobbying resulting in the passage of a bill which funded shelters for battered women and a bill which strengthened temporary restraining orders. There are similar organizations in most states and on the national level working toward passage of legislation to improve the status of battered women. Researching, writing, and lobbying for legislation is a very good way to effect change.

We must also educate the community because the criminal justice system just reflects societal attitudes. We need to get articles in the newspapers; we must talk to community groups; we must talk to men. We must change the climate, just as the climate was changed on the issue of rape a few years ago. We must use the same kind of educational process on battering and it is not a glamorous topic. It is not as much fun as running into the Federal Court and filing a suit, but it may, in the long run, be much more important.

The last, and probably the most extreme, action one can take is sue. I think every other remedy should be exhausted before doing that, because then an adversary position is created which may close off communication once a suit has been filed. I think a lawsuit may be very important because it makes us feel so strong. We are using the courts to say we are not going to take this anymore. We are being discriminated against, and we want the law enforcement system to protect us. While we might try everything else first, we must not be afraid to file a lawsuit if other methods fail.

Another method of pressuring for change has been used by women in Hayward, California. They said they were going to picket the home of batterers. They asked me to find out if this was protected speech or if they could be arrested. It is protected. Truth is an absolute defense in any lawsuit alleging slander or libel. These women were going to picket the man's job, his church, and generally make life uncomfortable for him. There are some very creative ways to deal with this whole issue, so think about a whole range of responses and share your creative solutions with people in other communities.

The Need to Bring About Change

One of the major problems we need to deal with is that our society does not view domestic violence as criminal conduct. Once again, remember that the criminal justice system simply reflects social views.

We have got to be able to give women support. We need to say to battered women, "Okay, it is going to be tough. You might have to be up on the witness stand and they might try to break you down but we will be there to help you stand up for yourself." We have to help women develop the strength to follow through on this so the attitudes of the criminal justice system and society can begin changing. Battering is not seen as a crime now and what we want to do is get people to see it as such. It is an assault; in many cases it is a felony assault.

On a more tangible level, women are being maimed and killed. Police are empowered to stop citizens from doing harm to property, persons, or society in general. Women who call the police for assistance expect that reality to be manifested for them. They expect the police to take these men out of the home and get them away from them and the police are not doing that. The criminal justice system is breaking down at that level. It is critical, then, that women work with the criminal justice system to change this reality.

When Martin Luther King was in the South, he was frequently asked "Why are you causing so much trouble? Why don't you be nice?" He said, "If I was nice, I would still be a slave. I would still be riding in the back of the bus. I would still be having to go in back doors." Battered women and their advocates must adopt the same approach. It is time to act in any way possible to stop the criminal assaults on women and get the criminal justice system to help women in the same way it helps other persons who are being assaulted.

MAKING THE LEGAL SYSTEM WORK
FOR BATTERED WOMEN

Sandra Blair

Introduction

The Legal System as a Reflection of Society

The legal system is one of the many institutions which composes society. The legal system is subject to all of the pressures of every other institution in society; it reflects our culture. Many times people think the legal system is the solution to all their problems. They think that somehow the legal system is going to help them and do things for them that no one else has been able to do, or that none of the other agencies or institutions in this society have been able to do. That may be true to a slight degree; however, the legal system is not the virtuous knight in shining armor rescuing all victims and righting all wrongs. It should, and it would be nice if it were so pure and untainted. Unfortunately, it has the same values which pervade our whole society and our society does not respect women. The legal system can reflect some of the worst aspects of society: distrust and disbelief of women. In understanding that the legal system is only a single institution out of many, we realize that today's improved laws can only have a small and superficial impact upon the cultural values of all of society. It is impossible to pass new laws that protect the victims of sexual inequality until society itself adopts those values and integrates them into its various institutions. So, keep in mind that as I discuss changing the legal system, I am only talking about superficial reforms which may help create basic cultural changes which in turn might lead to further reforms in the legal system. It is an interaction process between cultural attitudes and the legal system which we must recognize and use to create a system which is responsive to battered women.

The legal system traditionally lags behind social changes in our society. As cultural changes occur, the legal system will be altered in response to those changes in society. For instance, the publicity and education about battered women is beginning to make the legal system more responsive to the problems of these women. There have been laws on the books since the first criminal codes were written protecting women and all people from being beaten up by others. We all know these laws exist. It has only been in the last few years because of political pressure and because of new organizations that the legal system has begun to use those laws in an effective way to help battered women.

It is also important to recognize that, in spite of all of our idealism, the legal system does not generally protect the powerless. As an institution of our society, it reflects the power structure of society. The basic advocacy that goes on in the legal system is advocacy for the powerful; the powerless have to struggle to be represented and struggle to have people advocating for them. Battered women are certainly a powerless segment of society. They are powerless by virtue of being women and by virtue of their social and psychological conditions.

I will examine different aspects of the legal system to see how each aspect affects battered women. I will also discuss how to change the legal system to help prevent domestic violence and to help protect battered women.

The Laws

Laws That Create Programs

One kind of law we have is a law that creates programs. These laws tend to be almost, although not completely, self-implementing. For instance, we have laws that fund shelters for battered women and fund conferences about battered women. These are now part of the legal system in our society. These laws are usually approved by legislatures when interested groups lobby and create pressure for their passage. This is a relatively easy way for interested groups to help battered women. These laws are administered by agencies, but the agencies tend to have a very small role in the programs themselves: that is, they give out the money and monitor programs which are run and administered fairly independently. I believe we are in the beginning of a cycle of legislation of money for battered women's programs. So, we have a grassroots movement of people who are interested and who are lobbying to receive funds to implement programs. They are creating shelter organizations that will remain in existence for many years. These shelters are also influencing other helping agencies in our society: mental health units, welfare agencies, family service organizations, and parts of the legal system such as the police, the district attorneys, judges, and private lawyers. These program-funding laws are an important part of the legal system.

An important item to recognize is that at the beginning of the funding cycle, people in helping agencies and people creating shelters tend to be very enthusiastic and innovative, and therefore are extremely effective. It is critical that these grassroots persons, shelters, and organizations not become bureaucratized.

Programs become bureaucratized when the people in charge get used to doing things a certain way and become afraid of changing these routines. Programs become bureaucratized when the routines are so settled that they become more important than the goals of the program. Keeping the program in existence becomes a priority and the effectiveness of the program (the goal of helping people) becomes less important. Unfortunately, the phenomenon of bureaucratization often occurs, and it has stopped many established agencies from responding to the needs of battered women, simply because they have never done so in the past and are afraid to begin a new, unfamiliar service.

Some programs avoid bureaucratization by allowing people outside the staff of the program to make decisions. Often this takes the form of a community advisory board. Another way to counter bureaucratization is to make sure that the people being served have a concrete way of having input on program decisions. That means the battered women themselves help to develop the programs set up to serve them. Hopefully, the shelters will remain responsive and innovative even as they become more established in our society.

Criminal Laws

The second kind of law that we have in this society is the criminal law. These laws can be thought of as the clout laws. That is, there is a punishment attached to disobeying the law. In a library there are 40 to 50 volumes of California law. For example there is the commercial code, the welfare and institutions code, the revenue and taxation code, the evidence code. But the criminal code differs from all other laws if disobeyed.

Criminal law provides a punishment of loss of freedom. That is, the breaker of a criminal law can go to jail. Breaking other kinds of laws have different results. Criminal laws in our society hold up an ideal standard of behavior: if things were the way we think they should be, then we would not have a need for criminal laws. They would simply exist in case people wanted to read about what one is not supposed to do. Most criminal laws are obeyed not because people are looking over their shoulders and trying to decide whether they will be caught or whether they will be punished, but they are obeyed because we grow up believing certain behaviors are right. For those who do not believe in the "right" behavior, then there is punishment at the end of the criminal law.

Criminal law may be legislated and passed by people who break those laws themselves, or who would break them given the opportunity. For instance, legislators in state capitals and in Washington, D.C., passed laws against taking bribes to influence legislation. We later discovered that some of the people voting for those laws were breaking them at the very time they voted for them. If Lenore Walker's statistics are correct that in one out of two families there is battering going on, then it is quite probable that some of the people passing laws against domestic violence are themselves batterers. But the very passage of these laws against battering is important. It demonstrates that a significant number of women have begun the slow process of changing societal attitudes regarding what is acceptable behavior of men toward them.

We already have many criminal laws that should have adequately protected battered women. There are laws against using deadly weapons, or even possessing some dangerous weapons; there are laws against hitting other people, beating other people, or hurting other people; there are laws against child stealing and child abuse, which are often associated with wife beating and family battering situations; and we have specific laws against spouse beating. We also have laws against trespassing which can be utilized in an unmarried battering situation.

Civil Laws

A third kind of law is civil law, the bulk of which deal with relationships between people. Money is usually the incentive for not breaking civil laws. For example, if a milk distributor does not put enough cream in the milk and it falls below the legal requirements for homogenized milk, that distributor will be brought into court and fined.

Divorce laws are civil laws which regulate the division of property, support, and child custody between a wife and husband. Restraining orders are civil laws which are supposed to maintain a peaceful status quo during this process of division and separation. Restraining orders are often granted in the midst of a separation of a husband and wife. These orders attempt to forbid behavior that would not ordinarily occur except for the stress of the divorce. In order to keep the situation peaceful, there could be a restraining order saying that neither person is supposed to annoy the other in any way. That would take care of telephone calls at 2 a.m., camping out on the sidewalk in front of the house, and other disruptive behavior. That is the main thrust behind restraining orders—to maintain the civil peace.

Agencies That Enforce Criminal Laws

Now that I have outlined three types of laws in this society, let us take a look at the agencies which implement and enforce the criminal law. Basically, those agencies are the police, the district attorney's office, and the courts. The job of all these agencies is to advocate for a peaceful society and to maintain order. The people in these agencies, as the rest of us, are influenced by the beliefs and the attitudes toward women and families which affect the rest of our culture. How they do their job, then, depends on several factors. One factor is how they are influenced by these cultural beliefs. Another factor affecting how people in these agencies work is the policy of their particular agency regarding what is important. As each agency has developed and grown and learned to do its job, informal rules and beliefs have grown up regarding what is an important part of that job and what is not. The third factor to look at when we are trying to change the way those jobs are done is how the rewards are given out: when are employees in one of those agencies patted on the back for doing a good job and when are they ignored. As we look at each agency, then, we will look at these factors specifically as they affect behavior toward battered women.

Police

The police department is the agency that does the dirty work in the criminal system. They are out there on the line to protect the rest of us. In fact, they sometimes refer to themselves as the "thin blue line between chaos and order." What they do is to funnel cases into the District Attorney's Office and then into the courts. They can choose whether or not to begin a case, but they do not finish it. They can only start it by making an arrest.

Within the police department, what is a glamorous job? A glamorous, exciting job is catching bank robbers, murderers, and other "serious" criminals. That is what the medals are given out for. That is what police officers are promoted for. A good arrest, or a "good pinch," is catching the person that society believes is a bad person. Breaking up a family fight is not a "good pinch." Arresting a man who has been beating his wife, or the woman he lives with, is not something that an officer gets a medal for at the end of the year. We must change this reward system to include arresting batterers. Because the police are supposed to be advocates against violence against all people, this advocacy must extend to battered women. Until the reward system is changed, police officers will not be putting their energy into domestic violence cases. They may sometimes do it, but it is not going to be the kind of thing they go home and study. Nor do they race to be the first car on the scene after hearing a domestic violence radio call, as they do for other crimes.

In general, wife battering is not a crime that is thought of as seriously punishable by most of society. Convicts, locked behind bars, are not generally considered to include men whose only crime was that they beat up their wife or girlfriend. Police officers therefore get neither praise nor promotions for such arrests. They are both subtly and overtly encouraged to arrest in cases in which a conviction and sentencing will be imposed. So, if we want to change, or begin to change, police departments so they are better advocates for women, we can begin through political pressure on department policies regarding domestic violence. We must change public opinion so that men battering women will be a punishable crime and will be seen as something a bad person does that should not be done, and for which the police should make an arrest.

Another means of affecting police departments is to have feminist advocates within the department. People who will go to the scene with the police and interpret what is going on to the police, explain what is going on to the victims, and advocate arrest and jail when that is appropriate. Someone is needed who has feminist values and can work with the police without adopting their outlook. Whether the advocates should be part of the department is problematic. If they are part of the department, they will probably have more respect from the police officers. In other words, we need more feminist police officers on the street. The other side of this issue, however, is that as they become incorporated into the department, they will also most likely begin to adopt the values of the department. They will also be hired as entry-level police officers, which means they will not be the ones making policy within the department for a number of years.

Perhaps the best solution is to have feminist police officers on the street as well as a separate unit within the department which is both independent from and integral to the department specifically to serve as a feminist advocacy unit for battered women.

If there are going to be special units, however, they must be prestigious units: units that police officers want to be in, units that are respected within the police department, units in which officers are rewarded for doing a good job.

Another suggestion, of course, is education for the entire police department. The danger of designating special units to deal with battering is that battering becomes the problem of this specialized unit and nobody else has to worry about it. We know that battering is endemic throughout this society. There are calls coming in from all parts of the city, all hours of the day and night. All police officers have to respond to these situations, both within homes and on the streets, so there is a real need to educate all officers and to insist that each officer is responsible for responding appropriately to a battering incident.

In order to make changes in an institution, one must make institutional changes: if police officers are rewarded for making a good arrest, then we are changing the value of that type of arrest in the officer's mind. We are changing the values of the society. Research tells us that personal attitudes change when we force behavior to change in order to get rewards. Psychologists call this the "reduction of cognitive dissonance": that is, one begins believing in those behaviors one is forced to exhibit. This information can and should be used to change institutions within the criminal justice system. The best way to see this happen is for women and men to organize and put pressure on institutions to make those changes.

District Attorneys

Now let us look at the District Attorney's Office. After the police have done their job, the District Attorney's Office decides what, if anything, to do with the arrest. If there has not been an arrest, the police may have written up an incident report and given it to the District Attorney, or the woman may go directly to the District Attorney following advice from the police department. So there are three possible situations upon which the District Attorney may be asked to make a decision: an arrest, a police report, or a woman's request. If we have a police department which has been sensitized and sees battered women as an important problem, but the District Attorney is still not taking it seriously, we have gotten nowhere. If the police are rewarded only within their department but get no assistance from the District Attorney, they will most likely not continue working on battered women cases because they are not getting the external rewards of convictions and sentences. District Attorneys, remember, are agents of the state. Their job is to enforce the criminal law for the state, for the peace and order of the whole society. They are not an attorney for the victim and although they often view themselves as helping the victim, their first responsibility is to society. They are officers of the court and are committed to their particular District Attorney's Office and the policies of that office regarding what is the best way to promote order. They are also much more overtly political than the police department.

District Attorneys are usually elected or appointed by elected politicians. They are expected to be responsive to the populace. Police departments, on the other hand, are supposedly more removed, more neutral, and not influenced by politics. The District Attorney's Office can admit publicly that they are there to serve the public and if the public does not like what they are doing the District Attorney can be replaced by a new District Attorney who will be more responsive to people. The District Attorney's Office decides on what crimes they are going to expend their resources, their energy, their staff in preparing good cases for trial and getting convictions and sentences. This is the job of the District Attorney's Office.

The District Attorney also has complete discretion in choosing which crimes to pursue. You cannot go to a private attorney and ask that attorney to put somebody in jail or to invoke the criminal law. Only the District Attorney's Office can invoke the criminal law, so they are a very crucial institution when we are talking about advocacy for the victims of battering. They are the ones who pick up where the police have left off and go into the courts. As the police, they are also caught up in notions of what are glamorous crimes and what are not. They have to decide what offenses are important to the public; what they are going to get public acclaim for pursuing. In some ways they are even more interested in getting acclaim, because they are more political and depend on the public for retaining their jobs.

There are crimes in our society we do not think of as major crimes, although we do consider them serious and the District Attorney's Office sees these acts as a priority and pursues them. For instance, although it may not be thought of as a major crime, drunk driving is something that the public is generally concerned about. If the public thought the District Attorney's Office was letting drunk drivers go free, they would get upset and within a short time drunken driving would be treated in a different way. Shoplifting is also something people do not get excited about the way they get excited about a bank robbery or a murder, but most people would agree that shoplifters should be punished and would get upset if the District Attorney's Office said they were going to let it go. District Attorney's Offices, in general, have a long way to go. They could bring battering to the level of shoplifting and drunk driving if people were willing to influence them in a public, systematic way. This requires, of course, that the public see battering as a serious crime and demand that the District Attorney fully prosecute batterers. If they do not prosecute such cases, they should be publicly criticized, particularly around election time.

Most District Attorney's Offices now treat battered women victims differently from other victims of crime. They are suspicious that a battered woman will later be reluctant to testify so they demand written statements and medical evidence of the crime before filing charges against the perpetrator (batterer). Even when charges are filed, they will drop or dismiss these charges if the victim later changes her mind. This is different from the way other victims are treated. Other victims are not routinely asked to sign written statements before the charges are filed. And once the District Attorney's Office files charges for other crimes, they will pursue the criminal regardless of the victim's desires. For example, if my neighbor sets my house on fire and I later decide I do not want the person prosecuted, the District Attorney's Office will not listen to me. They will perceive their duty as enforcing the law against arson for the good of society. They will use the legal process (a subpoena) to compel me to testify if I am reluctant to do so. District Attorney's Offices must be compelled to protect battered women as they protect other victims of violent crimes.

One way we could affect changes in both the police departments and the District Attorney's Office is through legislation. A law could be enacted requiring that the police department write a report on all domestic violence calls. If there is no report the District Attorney has no information to act upon. The better the report, and the more cooperative and available the victim, the more the District Attorney has to work with. Although District Attorney's Offices do have investigative staffs, they are very small and they expect the police department to do most of the investigative work. The reports, therefore, should be thorough reports that explain the situation as best as possible. The police should have gathered as much evidence as possible at the scene and include that information in the report.

A second way we could affect District Attorney's Offices is through lay advocates. The District Attorney's Office is an excellent place for lay advocates and should be seriously considered and attempted. There are different problems in the District Attorney's Office than in the police department, where there are concerns about physical safety and liability for lay advocates. The District Attorney's Office is in an office setting: they gather facts, interview people, go to court. These are safe tasks and it is very easy to train lay people to gather facts, to prepare cases for trial, to speak to victims, and to prepare victims for trial.

Advocates in the District Attorney's Office can be helpful for a number of other very important reasons. They should be able to give the victims the support they need to break out of the cycle of violence that Dr. Walker and others talk about. Perhaps if we have advocates working directly with the victim we will be less likely to encounter situations in which the woman drops the charges and returns home because she feels she has no better alternative. Furthermore, if she does drop the charges and return home there will be less anger from the District Attorney since it has not been his/her time that was spent with the victim but the advocate's time. These advocates in the District Attorney's Office would know about shelters, counseling programs, and places to hide: the information would be there and they would not simply be talking to the victim once and saying "well come back in two months and there will be a pretrial hearing and we'll decide whether to take this to court or not." The District Attorney simply does not have the resources the way they are currently staffed and funded to do what an advocate unit could do.

A third and major change needed within the District Attorney's Office is to develop a new understanding of what is a triable offense. District Attorneys will only pursue what they consider to be triable offenses—offenses which juries will convict if the case comes to trial. Even though most cases do not come to trial, the standard the District Attorney uses in deciding whether to prosecute is what would happen if this case went in front of a jury. If the decision is that a jury would not convict, the charge is lowered, plea bargained, or dropped. The District Attorneys often say a jury will never convict on a family matter so they do not take them to court. This is beginning to change, partly as a result of publicity, political pressure, and the awareness about battered women which the shelters movement has been able to disseminate throughout the public. As evidence of that, I would point to the recent acquittals of battered women who killed their husbands in self-defense. There have been several all over the country.[1] Of course, part of putting on a trial is explaining to the jury the context within which the crime occurred; and if it occurred in an uncommon context, then more information should be brought to the jury and they should be helped to understand what makes the case different. I think we are beginning to get juries who will see wife battering as triable and convictable cases if we can train District Attorneys how to present the cases.

We have to make battered women convictions as good as other types of convictions, such as convictions for assaulting a stranger. We have to remember the way the District Attorney decides to prosecute and gets a conviction. In other words, the police will make good arrests if the District Attorney goes ahead and utilizes all the evidence the police have gathered to get a conviction. Those two actions go together and one cannot just put pressure on one agency without also working with the other agency. The police may be more easily developed into allies because they see people as bad who assault others and are violent. They see violence a lot and it is not much of an extension for them to see this violent person as bad. It is harder for the District Attorney because by the time one gets to the District Attorney's Office, people are dressed in suits and on their good behavior and somehow it is harder for batterers to be seen as a criminal group.

The District Attorney's Office is accountable to the public and what we need is a better system of accountability in terms of domestic violence. We need statistics. How many arrests were made that they did not follow up on, how many victims backed out, what happened to the cases. Cases need to be tracked by outside agencies so the public has the necessary data to use in developing political pressure to change District Attorney's Offices.

The Courts

The courts, then, are the last institution in the legal system and they are there as neutral arbitrators—after the police have arrested and the District Attorney has brought charges. They are advocates for the state: not just protecting the victim but as an agency ensuring against violence in our society.

In the courts, the batterer will have a trial before a judge (and sometimes a jury) and the batterer will have his own lawyer. The judge will make important decisions: how the trial is to be conducted, what evidence is proper, what instructions the jury gets, and what sentence the batterer receives if he is convicted of a crime.

Judges and other courtroom personnel such as the clerks, court reporter, and bailiff, all create an attitude in the courtroom which affects the proceedings. If, for instance, they find the battering situation humorous and make jokes, then the batterer and his attorney will use the situation to lessen or escape punishment. The judge may see this matter as one which should not be taking court time, one which does not belong in the criminal system. These attitudes will influence the crucial decisions made by the judge during the trial.

Judges, as police and District Attorneys, may see battering as a personal rather than a social problem. They may wonder if the woman caused the problem or provoked the attack. They may wonder why she did not simply leave or divorce her husband. The judge is likely to be impatient with the problem, thinking it is a waste of public time and money to have a trial when "more serious" cases are waiting for courtrooms.

Specific educational programs for judges and other court personnel about battered women are a good starting point for changing attitudes in the courtroom. If the judge better understands the psychological dynamics and physical danger of the battering situations, he is more likely to treat it as a serious matter.

Judges also can approve diversion. This is a procedure in which an accused person can attend a counseling program instead of going to trial and facing a conviction if the person does not have a prior criminal record. If there were more alternative programs for batterers, judges would be more comfortable treating them as criminals who need help in order to reform their behavior, rather than simply sentencing them to jail time.

We need new and different probation programs. Probation can be ordered after a person is instructed to attend a rehabilitative program in his community. Often jail time is used as a threat—the guilty person will go to jail if he violates the rules of his probation. We have alcoholic rehabilitation programs: we could have wife beater rehabilitation programs. These programs should be available immediately after a first altercation. They should not be the last recourse after a man has brutally beaten his partner; they should start before the beatings become frequent and/or serious.

If we had rehabilitation programs for the less than "serious battering," perhaps it would make a difference. A model could be the program of driving school used for speeders. Instead of being fined they are sent to driving school and are shown pictures of horrible accident scenes. Well, why not do that with battering? Why not take somebody who has just slapped a woman around a couple of times and show him the results of that, show him what ultimately happens. Get people in there who have been seriously battered and talk about it. Discussion groups and counseling groups in which men encourage each other to change this violent behavior could be another therapeutic mode.

These are all actions the criminal justice system could, and should, take. I believe wife battering needs to remain in the jurisdiction of the criminal justice system because it is a crime and should be handled as one, although it need not necessarily be handled by jail sentences. I do not believe that individual women who have been battered should bear the burden of hiring private attorneys in order that their needs can be met through the civil courts. We can now look at what the civil courts can currently do for a battered woman, keeping in mind that such cases should probably ideally be dealt with in the criminal courts.

Civil Laws for Battered Women

Civil laws, as I said earlier, are laws that are supposed to maintain the status quo: to maintain the peace where there is not peace and where there is possibility that there might not be peace. The idea behind civil laws is that people are law abiding and when a judge tells them to stop doing something, they will obey that judge's orders. Restraining orders, in that sense, are effective only to the extent that a person is intimidated by the court's authority. The problem is that when a man is violent and is battering his wife, restraining orders usually do not work. Many men feel that no one is going to tell them what to do to their wife, not even a judge. Other men are so locked into a pattern of violence that even a court order cannot suddenly curtail their behavior.

We can get restraining orders, especially in a divorce situation, that require a man to leave the home, because of the likelihood of further physical harm to the children or wife. This is a satisfactory standard to use for having somebody ordered out of their own home. In some states we now have laws with which even the nonmarried can be ordered out of the home in the same way. These orders are most effective when the situation is merely bad, but not physically violent. These are people who will usually comply with the orders. When a woman asks an attorney for a restraining order after having suffered a history of domestic violence, it will probably be ineffective. There already is a law against beating your wife and a restraining order is simply another law. If the man is not concerned about assault laws he probably will not care much about the temporary restraining order either.

There are two primary legal mechanisms for enforcing civil orders. One is contempt of court. If a person disobeys a civil restraining order in which a judge has ordered the man to stay away from the woman, it is a contempt of court. The woman now has to go back to her attorney and fill out new papers for contempt of court. Those papers must then be served on the violator, which can sometimes be difficult. The papers say that there is a hearing scheduled, usually three or four weeks later. At that hearing the judge is to decide, beyond a reasonable doubt, if the order was broken. If the judge finds that the person disobeyed the civil order of the court, then (s)he can order a jail sentence. The punishment is up to five days in jail for one act of contempt. If there were several acts, there could be a several-day sentence. It is extremely unusual in the civil system for the judge to exercise this power and put the person in jail for contempt of court. The judge's attitude toward this violation of a civil order is similar to the criminal situation discussed above—(s)he may feel it is very serious and enforce the law conscientiously or (s)he may find it humorous and thereby give implicit, and sometimes explicit, approval to the violator's behavior. Once in a while a judge does order jail for someone who violates a civil order, but it is most frequently a result of failure to pay child support rather than a result of violating a temporary restraining order.

The second way to enforce the civil order is through police enforcement. It is a crime in California to disobey a civil order, even though what was ordered may not normally be a crime. For instance, if someone is ordered to leave her/his home, then she/he is under a court order to leave the house. Ordinarily, it would not be a crime to be there, but now it is a crime because of the order. If the person is at the door, they are already committing a crime—one does not have to wait until there has been a beating. Again, police give these acts very low priority. They do not understand them, so they tell women to go see their attorney because it is a civil matter. Better education for the police in this matter would be very helpful. Police could develop a system to verify the existence of temporary restraining orders. Currently police departments have systems to verify outstanding warrants: the officer in the field can detain a person, check to see if he/she is wanted on a warrant, then arrest the person if there is such a warrant. Restraining orders could be incorporated into this system easily by most police departments. It is a way to encourage the police to enforce the orders: it is also an excellent way to educate them about those orders and what they mean and to integrate these cases into the criminal system.

I would like to close with an idea, which is to form new and hopefully temporary institutions of advocacy for battered women, perhaps along the lines of Child Protective Services. It could be initiated through the police, the District Attorney, or through a telephone call, just like a crisis line. It would be made up of former battered women, social workers who are sensitive to domestic violence, attorneys, lay advocates who are familiar with family law and with the criminal and civil processes. These people would watch and monitor all cases: they would work with the police and the District Attorney's Office and would also serve in a watchdog capacity in terms of what agencies are doing. They would help prepare reports and charges and get expertise in those areas to make it easier for other agencies. They would be able to institute civil actions when appropriate and, of course, offer shelter and other resources to battered women. That, in my opinion, would be the best and most effective system of advocacy we could have right now to deal with battered women.

5

EXPERIENCES WITH AND
VIEWS ABOUT BATTERING
A Research Note

Donna M. Moore
Fran Pepitone-Rockwell

Introduction: The Conference and
the Questionnaire

In the spring of 1978, a conference entitled "Battered Women" was held on the campus of the University of California at Davis. The conference was prompted by extensive reading and requests for counseling on the part of the first author, who began to understand that this is one of the most frequent and least understood forms of violence against women. A planning committee was developed which consisted of persons in the fields of law enforcement, mental health, and education who had either had contact with battered women or who had a major interest in learning more about the issues involved. The conference was jointly sponsored by the Women's Resources and Research Center and University Extension at the University of California at Davis. Broad-scale publicity was given the conference to solicit participation by the university's students, women working in shelters, legislators, counselors, social service agency personnel, and branches of law enforcement. Because this was the first conference of its type held in California, an attempt was made to attract both male and female participants as well as a wide age range to gather information and impart concern over a broad range of persons. Workshop topics included information regarding the batterer, the battered, effects on children, the legal system, institutional sexism, sex-role stereotyping, crisis intervention, establishing a shelter, feminist analysis of wife beating, legislative changes and responses, personal support for the victim, social service agencies, and hospital emergency room staffs. A workshop was also held specifically for men on understanding and working with anger.

Four keynote speeches covered an overview of battering, a psychological analysis of the cycles of battering, the legal system, and information regarding how to create an advocacy system for battered women. Additionally, a panel of four battered women presented their experiences and information about both those factors which kept them in the battering situation and those which finally allowed them to leave. Each workshop was facilitated by two to four persons who were experienced and recognized as experts in the workshop topic area. Brochures listing workshops as well as the names and credentials of all facilitators were mailed to agencies and persons throughout the state to attract a heterogeneous group of participants and encourage interaction among professionals and lay persons.

In an attempt to look at experiences and views regarding battering and violence of persons attending such a conference, questionnaires (see Appendix D) were distributed on the morning of the third (and final) day of the conference. Participants were asked to complete the questions and leave the questionnaire in a box as they left. No time was designated to complete the questionnaire so those who completed the form did so by remaining for a few minutes after the closing speech. Persons who were willing to stay longer numbered 120, or 60.9% of the total conference attendance of 197.

The questionnaire had been designed by the authors to gather some preliminary data regarding the demographic characteristics of persons who would attend a three-day weekend workshop at personal expense on a topic which has so recently been recognized as relevant to both men and women and to a variety of professional fields. While the authors recognized that persons attending such an event would not be a random sample of the population, it seemed important to begin gathering some preliminary data. Further, we wanted to determine the experiences these persons may have had with violence and how they viewed battering. We felt that gathering such information might serve as a guide for others who later wished to conduct similar conferences, training programs, and research. In reviewing the pertinent literature, we determined that no one had designed any reliable test instruments on battering. It was our hope that our questionnaire might be seen as preliminary to the development of a reliable and valid instrument for measuring people's attitudes about battering. The data presented here need to be read keeping in mind that our sample was not representative and the instrument not validated but that they might serve as beginning information for those conducting research on battering.

Description of the Participants

Sex and Age

As can be seen from Table 1, 110 of the 120 persons responding were female (91.7%) and 10 were male (8.3%). These numbers would appear to be representative of all conference participants: although enrollment forms did not ask demographic information, visual impressions confirmed that we had an overwhelmingly female audience. While neither the percentage of 8.3, nor the absolute number of 10 respondents can be generalized to the larger male population, the authors feel it is important to keep male and female respondents separate in order to extricate differences in both experiences and viewpoints which might suggest areas for further research. We will, therefore, present the data throughout this chapter in a gender-segregated manner.

Table 1 also shows that most of the males (33.3%) were 24 years of age or younger, while the largest portion of females (31.8%) were between the ages of 25 and 29. Over half (58.9%) of the females were ages 25 to 34 although there were women ranging from under 20 years to over 50 years. Men also ranged from under 20 to over 40 with no male participants in the 50-year-old range.

Occupations

It would appear from Table 2 that the conference publicity did, indeed, attract a heterogeneous population. The largest percentage of females were students (29.09%), followed by social service workers (13.64%), psychologists or counselors and women's agency workers (this category includes rape counselors, battered women's shelter workers, women's advocates, and consultants regarding feminist issues), both at 12.73%; other (including housewives, secretaries, an author and a truck owner) representing 11.82%, medical (physicians and nurses) 8.18%, legal 6.36%, and educators 5.45%. The only field in which women were not represented was that of police work, one of the two largest groups of males in attendance.

Males were most heavily occupied in the fields of counseling and psychology and police work (30% each), followed by one student, one person working in a women's organization, one physician, and one educator. No men were in the social service or legal fields or in the miscellaneous other categories.

Overall, then, the largest single category of participants was students (27.5%) which was probably related to the location of the conference and the fact that the university students could enroll for $5, while it cost all others $40. In addition to students, the conference had a cross-representation of professionals from the fields of counseling, social services, and women's organizations, with lower numbers from the medical, police, legal, and educational fields.

TABLE 1
Gender and Age of Respondents[a]

Age	Female (N=110)		Male (N=10)		Total (N=120)
	N	%	N	%	N
20-24	18	(16.8)	3	(33 1/3)	21
25-29	34	(31.8)	1	(11.1)	35
30-34	29	(27.1)	2	(22.2)	31
35-39	11	(10.3)	2	(22.2)	13
40-49	10	(9.35)	1	(11.1)	11
50-59	5	(4.67)	–	–	5

a. Three female and one male respondents did not provide age data.

Education

It is clear from Table 3 that the educational level of participants was unusually high. There was only one female who had discontinued her education at the high school level, while no males had quit school that early. The majority of both women (71.96%) and men (60%) had completed either bachelor or master's degrees. The male and female respondents looked very similar with regard to educational level except that no men had quit after high shcool and there were no male lawyers represented, while there were three female lawyers. The important factor seems to be that overall these people were quite highly educated.

Reasons for Attending the Conference

The majority of participants (Table 4) attended the conference because it was related to their current job (35.05%). Other reasons listed were that the conference might give the person information which would be related to future job goals (19.21%), that the conference would help with academic endeavors (14.69%), that the person was interested in gathering more information regarding battering (22.60%), and personal reasons, which included having been battered or having friends

TABLE 2
Gender and Occupation of Respondents

Occupation	Female (N=110)		Male (N=10)		Total (N=120)	
	N	%	N	%	N	%
Student	32	(29.09)	1	(10)	33	(27.5)
Social service	15	(13.64)	–	–	15	(12.5)
Psychology/counselor	14	(12.73)	3	(30)	17	(14.16)
Women's agency workers	14	(12.73)	1	(10)	15	(12.5)
Other	13	(11.82)	–	–	13	(10.83)
Medical	9	(8.18)	1	(10)	10	(8.33)
Legal	7	(6.36)	–	–	7	(5.83)
Education	6	(5.45)	1	(10)	7	(5.83)
Police	–	–	3	(30)	3	(2.5)

who had been battered (8.47%). The most glaring differences between male and female participants were that no men attended for personal reasons, while 9.15% of the female respondents indicated such motives. A second major difference was that 20.12% of the females indicated that they had future job goals related to battering, while only 7.69% of the males gave such reasons for attending the conference.

Expectations for the Conference

Respondents were asked to indicate what their expectations had been for the conference and then to rate how well those expectations had been met. These questions were open-ended, allowing participants to provide their own reasons in any way they chose. Responses were then put into the 10 categories with three levels for meeting expectations which appear in Table 5. Three raters placed responses into the 10 categories and three expectation levels with an interrater reliability of .97 agreement about how to classify responses.

It would appear that the largest expectation of both men and women (44.57%) was to get general information regarding

TABLE 3
Education Level of Participants[a]

Education	Female (N=107)		Male (N=10)		Total (N=117)	
	N	%	N	%	N	%
High school	1	(0.93)	–	–	1	(0.8)
Some college	21	(19.63)	1	(10)	22	(18.8)
B.A./B.S.	39	(36.45)	3	(30)	42	(35.8)
M.A./M.S.	38	(35.51)	3	(30)	41	(35)
Ph.D.	3	(2.80)	2	(20)	5	(4.2)
M.D.	2	(1.87)	1	(10)	3	(2.5)
J.D.	3	(2.80)	–	–	3	(2.5)

a. Three women did not give educational data.

battering. Women's expectations were largely met (84.66%), 9.20% of their expectations were only partially met, and 6.13% went unmet. Men indicated that 75% of their expectations had been fully met, 16.66% partially met, and only 8.33% went unmet.

The major differences, by gender, between respondents were in the following categories: while 17 (10.43%) of the women had come expecting to obtain information regarding shelters, no men were interested in such information. Women were also interested in getting information regarding the characteristics of the batterer (3.06%), information regarding funding sources, and information regarding effects on children (.61% each), none of which seemed to interest men. Men, on the other hand, expressed the expectation (16.66%) that they would, and indeed did, find the conference giving antimale and antipolice attitudes to the participants. It is probably not coincidental that the two respondents who indicated these expectations (which were met) were themselves male police officers.

Overall, the only categories of expectations fully unmet were those respondents who had anticipated getting information regarding funding and the effects of battering on children.

It should also be added that 19 (17.27%) of the female respondents, but none of the male respondents, added extensive

TABLE 4
Major Factors for Attending Conference

Factor	Female (N=110)		Male (N=10)		Total (N=120)	
	N	%	N	%	N	%
Current job related	57	(34.76)	5	(38.46)	62	(35.03)
Future job related	33	(20.12)	1	(7.69)	34	(19.21)
Academic	24	(14.63)	2	(15.38)	26	(14.69)
Informational	35	(21.34)	5	(38.46)	40	(22.60)
Personal	15	(9.15)	–	–	15	(8.47)
Totals[a]	164		13		177	

a. Totals will exceed 120 because some respondents checked more than one category.

comments, unsolicited by the questionnaire, indicating that their expectations had been far exceeded and that the conference had been a major positive event for either their professional or personal growth.

In summarizing the foregoing information, it would appear that we have a largely female population of whom the majority are 25 to 34 years of age, professionally occupied, and well-educated. They attended this conference largely for career and informational purposes and came with expectations which were, for the most part, met by the workshops and speakers. Next we would like to look at the kind of experiences these people have had, either in childhood or adulthood, with regard to violence and battering.

Battering-Related Experiences of the Participants

This information was obtained through eight questions randomly spaced throughout the questionnaire. Data are presented, both in terms of absolute numbers and in percentages, by gender for each of the eight questions (Table 6). It should be noted that only on three of the eight questions did we obtain 120 responses.

TABLE 5
Expectations of the Participants for the Conference

Expectation	Female (N=110)			Male (N=10)			Total Expectations
	Expectations Met	Expectations Partially Met	Expectations Unmet	Expectations Met	Expectations Partially Met	Expectations Unmet	
To get general information re: battered women	68	3	2	4	—	1	78 (44.57%)
To locate resources	24	3	—	1	—	—	28 (16%)
Information re: counseling	18	—	—	1	1	—	19 (10.86%)
Information re: shelters	11	3	3	—	—	—	17 (9.71%)
To find solutions	9	1	2	1	1	—	14 (8%)
Information re: legal system	4	5	—	1	—	—	10 (5.71%)
Information re: batterers	4	—	1	—	—	—	5 (2.86%)
To hear antimale, antipolice attitudes	—	—	—	2	—	—	2 (1.14%)
Information re: funding	—	—	1	—	—	—	1 (0.57%)
Information re: children	—	—	1	—	—	—	1 (0.57%)
Totals[a]	138 (84.66%)	15 (9.20%)	10 (6.13%)	9 (75%)	2 (16.66%)	1 (8.33%)	175

a. Totals exceed 120 because respondents checked several categories.

TABLE 6
Experiences with and Fears about Battering

Experience		Frequently		Occasionally		Once		Never		Total	
		N	%	N	%	N	%	N	%	N	%
FEMALE (N=110)											
Battered as an adult	N=120	5	(4.5)	16	(14.5)	18	(16.4)	71	(64.5)	39	(35.4)
Battered during childhood	N=113	7	(6.8)	11	(10.7)	9	(8.7)	76	(73.8)	27	(26.2)
Witnessed battering during childhood	N=117	7	(6.5)	22	(20.6)	11	(10.3)	67	(62.6)	40	(37.4)
Have battered a spouse	N=117	–	–	6	(5.6)	8	(7.5)	93	(86.9)	14	(13.1)
Have battered a child	N=114	–	–	10	(9.6)	2	(1.9)	92	(88.5)	12	(11.5)
Have battered an animal	N=120	1	(0.9)	16	(14.5)	4	(3.6)	89	(80.9)	21	(19.1)
Fear being battered	N=120	17	(15.4)	57	(51.8)	18	(16.4)	18	(16.4)	92	(83.6)
Fear becoming a batterer	N=116	2	(1.9)	14	(13.2)	10	(9.4)	80	(75.5)	26	(24.5)
MALE (N=10)											
Battered as an adult	N=120	–	–	–	–	–	–	10	(100)	–	–
Battered during childhood	N=113	1	(10)	2	(20)	–	–	7	(70)	3	(30)
Witnessed battering during childhood	N=117	2	(20)	1	(10)	1	(10)	6	(60)	4	(40)
Have battered a spouse	N=117	–	–	–	–	–	–	10	(100)	–	–
Have battered a child	N=114	–	–	–	–	–	–	10	(100)	–	–
Have battered an animal	N=120	–	–	2	(20)	1	(10)	7	(70)	3	(30)
Fear being battered	N=120	–	–	2	(20)	–	–	8	(80)	2	(20)
Fear becoming a batterer	N=116	–	–	–	–	1	(10)	9	(90)	1	(10)

It seems that the male respondents have led relatively violence-free lives: none admitted to having ever battered their own spouse nor to having been battered by their spouse; they also had never battered a child. A few (30%) had, however, been battered as a child and witnessed battering as a child. A few (30%) also indicated having perpetrated violence against an animal more than once. Perhaps the most interesting percentages, although one must keep the absolute numbers in mind, are those relating to the fear of either battering or being battered: while only 10% of the men indicated they had ever been afraid of hurting a woman, 20% indicated that they had occasionally been afraid that they would be hurt (physically) by a female.

Women's experiences look somewhat different: they had both been battered by their spouses (35.4%) and had perpetrated violence against the spouse (13.08%)—it should not be surprising that the number of those who had beaten their spouses was lower than that of those who had been battered. Additionally, 11.54% admitted to beating a child once or occasionally, while 19.09% indicated they had been violent with an animal. Female respondents had seen violence among family members during childhood (37.38%), as had the men. As with the men, the figures for fear of battering and fear of being battered were very telling: 83.64% feared physical violence at the hands of men, and 24.53% feared that they would indeed hurt a man physically. It is particularly interesting to notice that in both men and women, although the actual experiences with violence, either as a child or as an adult, were fairly low (one could perhaps argue that anything at all is not low enough), the *fear* of both experiencing and of perpetrating physical harm on persons of the opposite sex was quite high. Both men (23.28%) and women (24.53%) were far less worried about personally becoming batterers than they were of being the recipients of violence (83.64% for women, 78.33% for men).

Only 13.08% of the women and none of the men admitted to battering a spouse, and 11.54% of the women and none of the men admitted to battering a child. However, 19.09% of the women and 30% of the men had battered animals.

Now we would like to look at how participants regard battering, particularly with an eye to how experiences might be consistent or inconsistent with the opinions participants held about battering.

Causes for Battering

As can be seen from Table 7, both men and women (65.22%) tend to believe that battering occurs, and continues to occur, because of the socialization patterns experienced by both partners in a battering home.

Men's responses regarding why battering occurs fell into only two response categories: socialization patterns (90%) and other (10%), which included poor parenting for the male child and poor communication between the adult couple. Although the majority of female responses (62.86%) attributed battering to socialization patterns, women also believed that male superiority in this society (18.09%) and cultural attitudes regarding the male prerogative (18.09%) contributed to the syndrome of battering. It is interesting to note that no male used either of these response alternatives. It should be noted that neither males nor females believed that the woman's attitude or behavior contributed to the onset of battering.

Responses regarding the reasons for battering continuing looked very similar to the responses for it occurring in the first place. The questionnaire design did yield some additional information, however; respondents were asked to consider the responses of public agencies and the courts—alternatives which had not been provided in the question regarding the initial causes of battering. Males attributed the causes for battering continuing to socialization (58.33%), as did female respondents (46.66%). Both males and females felt that the responses of public agencies (male 16.66%, female 20%) contributed to battering continuing. Again, male respondents did

TABLE 7
Major Reasons Battering Occurs and Continues

Reason	Female (N=105)		Male (N=10)		Total (N=115)	
	N	%	N	%	N	%
Major reason battering occurs						
Socialization	66	(62.86)	9	(90)	75	(65.22)
Male superiority in society	19	(18.09)	–	–	19	(16.52)
Male attitudes toward women	19	(18.09)	–	–	19	(16.52)
Women's attitudes or behavior	–	–	–	–	–	–
Other (poor parenting, poor communication)	1	(.95)	1	(10)	2	(1.74)
All of the above	6	(5)	3	(2.5)	9	(7.5)
Major reason battering continues						
Socialization	63	(46.66)	7	(58.33)	70	(47.62)
Responses of public agencies	27	(20)	2	(16.66)	29	(19.73)
Responses of courts	11	(8.15)	–	–	11	(7.48)
The man's attitudes	9	(6.66)	–	–	9	(6.12)
The woman's attitudes	6	(4.44)	–	–	6	(4.08)
Other (cultural acceptability; all; situational stress)	1	(.74)	1	(8.33)	2	(1.36)
All five categories[a]	18	(13.33)	2	(16.66)	20	(13.61)

a. Respondents checked more than one category.

not believe that the courts, the man's attitudes, or the woman's attitudes affected battering, while a few female respondents felt that all three factors contributed to battering (courts 8.15%, man's attitudes 6.66%, woman's attitudes 4.44%). It is particularly important to note that female respondents did not feel that a woman's attitudes were the cause for the onset of battering but some (4.44%) did feel the woman's attitudes could contribute to the continuation of battering once it had begun.

Overall, respondents simply felt that the socialization patterns which contribute to men's and women's attitudes about themselves, about the other sex, and about acceptable sex-role behavior were the single most significant cause both for the onset of battering (65.22%) and for the continuation of such behavior (47.62%). The most significant differences in views between the sexes is that men did not feel that male superiority in society or male attitudes toward women or the responses of the courts affected battering, while females did. Additionally, a few women believed that a woman's attitudes can lead to continuation of battering although not to initial onset; men did not feel the woman's attitudes play a role in either area. It seems clear to the authors that these questions were far too simple to get at the salient issues about why battering begins or continues, although the preliminary data would seem to indicate that both sexes will blame socialization patterns, while only women are willing to point to a male-dominated society.

Helping the Victim

There was a series of four questions, summarized in Table 8, designed to obtain information regarding attitudes toward helping the victim, and particularly to force some choices between female and male victims, female and child abuse victims, and public versus private handling of battering problems. It did not come as a surprise to the authors that these four questions elicited the largest number of narrative responses (unsolicited by the questionnaire), which expressed dismay that we would ask anyone to make such choices and hostility that such a choice would be considered, in addition to thoughtfulness and concern. The single largest voluntary narrative was given by 25 persons (24 women, 1 man) who indicated that they thought we needed to work with *both* abused women and children and that they should not be asked to make such a choice.

The first item in this group stated that while it was important to assist battered women, it was not important to work with male batterers. Male and female respondents alike disagreed with this item with 95.76% of all persons answering "Disagree" or "Strongly Disagree." The tone of the conference as a whole, and those individual speakers and participants with whom the authors talked, was a genuine concern that the feminist movement address itself to male batterers also. Indeed, if we are living in a male-oriented culture and if men do retain the power and decision making roles, it becomes imperative to include them in the solutions, which means providing services to batterers also. The respondents seemed to reflect this view which is not surprising given the atmosphere within which the problem had been discussed for the previous three days.

The second and fourth questions in this series addressed themselves to giving battered women information regarding their alternatives and whether (once we give the information) the battering should become a public one or retain its private nature. The first of these two questions elicited very little disagreement either within or between the sexes. A full 100% of both males and females agreed that we must give women information regarding their alternatives. Once such information was given, however, most respondents believed that the problem should not be a private affair to be resolved between the two people involved. In other words, this is a public problem and our responsibility goes beyond information giving. While only female respondents (4.55%) felt that battering is a private affair to be resolved between the partners, the majority of both men and women (90.84%) felt it should *not* remain a family affair.

TABLE 8
Helping the Victims

Factor	Strongly Agree	Agree	Undecided	Disagree	Strongly Disagree	Total
"While it is important to provide help for the battered woman, nothing needs to be done to assist the male batterer"						
Female N	—	1	3	24	80	108
Female %	—	(.93)	(2.78)	(22.22)	(74.07)	
Male N	—	—	1	1	8	10
Male %	—	—	(10)	(10)	(80)	
Combined Totals (N=118) 95.76% Disagree or Strongly Disagree						
"It is important to provide information regarding alternatives to battered women"						
Female N	105	3	—	—	—	108
Female %	(97.2)	(2.78)	—	—	—	
Male N	9	1	—	—	—	10
Male %	(90)	(10)	—	—	—	
Combined Totals (N=118) 100% Agree or Strongly Agree; 96.6% Strongly Agree						

TABLE 8 (Continued)

Factor	Strongly Agree	Agree	Undecided	Disagree	Strongly Disagree	Total
"It is more important to work with abused children than with battered women"						
Female N	1	6	10	51	29	97
Female %	(1.03)	(6.18)	(10.31)	(52.58)	(29.90)	
Male N	2	1	3	4	–	10
Male %	(20)	(10)	(30)	(40)	–	
Combined Totals N=107a						
"While we should give women information regarding their alternatives, family violence should remain a private affair to be resolved by the parties involved"						
Female N	5	–	8	22	75	110
Female %	(4.55)	–	(7.27)	(20)	(68.18)	
Male N	–	–	1	4	5	10
Male %	–	–	(10)	(40)	(50)	
Combined Totals (N=120) 66.67% Strongly Disagree; 24.17% Disagree						

a. In addition to the 107 responses recorded, 25 persons (24 women, 1 man) indicated we must work with *both* abused women and battered children; 5 respondents wrote notes indicating they felt this was a poor question.

The final item in this series stated that it was more important to help abused children than battered women. As indicated earlier, this particular item elicited a great deal of written narrative. Generally, however, although respondents did not like the choice, it is interesting to note the overall results. Men tended to agree that children are more important (30%), while women tended to disagree that children are more important (82.48%). Remembering that our number of male respondents is small, it would appear that this issue of prioritizing services to abused children and battered women warrants further research, particularly in view of the fact that most funding agencies continue to be managed and controlled by males. If, indeed, women feel that priorities need to be shifted, we will need to persuade the decision makers who may be males and who might very well consider children more important. This issue will become increasingly important as monies for social service agencies become harder to obtain.

Police Response

It is interesting that in view of the previous items which indicated respondents did not feel battering should be a private affair, Table 9 shows that the largest percentage of persons felt that when police officers do not respond adequately to a battering situation, it is because the officer has the attitude that domestic violence is a private affair. Overall, there seemed to be no major disagreements between male and female respondents on this item. Generally, people seemed to feel that the lack of adequate police response could come from all of the items listed, although the single largest response (35.68%) was "the attitude that it is a private affair."

Social Service Agencies

Overall, both male and female respondents agreed (83.33%) that public social service agencies such as medical facilities, physicians, police departments, and others need to have a

TABLE 9
Police Response

	Female (N=110)		Male (N=10)		Total [a] (N=120)	
	N	%	N	%	N	%
"When an inadequate response of law enforcement officers occurs, it is due to":						
Fear of injury	22	(12.64)	1	(9.09)	23	(12.43)
Lack of training	31	(17.82)	2	(18.18)	33	(17.84)
Attitude that it is a private affair	63	(36.21)	3	(27.27)	66	(35.68)
Attitude re: male prerogatives	33	(18.97)	1	(9.09)	34	(18.38)
All of the above	24	(13.79)	2	(18.18)	26	(14.05)
Other (inadequate number of officers; the woman's attitudes)	1	(.57)	2	(18.18)	1	(.54)
Total	174		11		185	

a. Respondents may have checked more than one category.

protocol for reporting battering similar to the one currently being used in many states for reporting incidents of abused children. They also agreed (84.61%) that such reporting should be made mandatory by law, similar to the mandatory reporting of suspected child abuse. And finally, they strongly agreed (95.76%) that we should make educational training about battering mandatory for medical, legal, law enforcment, and other public social service agency personnel in order to better equip them with information regarding both the problems as well as possible solutions.

Visitation Rights

Battered women have often reported that child visitation is problematic due to the additional psychological stress put on them by the batterer's arrival to pick up children for visitation and the fear that he will not return children or will abuse them.

TABLE 10
Social Service Agencies

Factor	Strongly Agree	Agree	Undecided	Disagree	Strongly Disagree	Total
Need protocol for battered women similar to the one for abused children						
Female N	57	29	11	5	2	104
Female %	(54.81)	(27.88)	(10.58)	(4.81)	(1.92)	
Male N	4	5	1	–	–	10
Male %	(40)	(50)	(10)			
Combined Totals (N=114) 83.33% Agree or Strongly Agree						
Public agencies should be required to report battering just like child abuse						
Female N	61	30	12	3	1	107
Female %	(57.01)	(28.04)	(11.21)	(2.80)	(.93)	
Male N	6	2	2	–	–	10
Male %	(60)	(20)	(20)			
Combined Totals (N=117) 84.61% Agree or Strongly Agree						
Educational training regarding battered women should be required						
Female N	90	13	3	–	2	108
Female %	(83.33)	(12.04)	(2.78)		(1.85)	
Male N	7	3	–	–	–	10
Male %	(70)	(30)				
Combined Totals (N=118) 95.76% Agree or Strongly Agree						

We asked participants, therefore, if they felt visitation rights should be denied the battering spouse. An equal number of persons (40.87%) were in the agreement or undecided categories, while only 18.26% felt that visitation should not be denied. Not surprisingly, however, there were some gender differences on this question (Table 11). An equal number of men (30%) agreed and disagreed with this idea—that is, they were not unanimous in how this problem should be dealt with. Women, on the other hand, were more in favor of denying visitation rights (41.90%) than not (17.14%), although overall 40.95% of the female respondents were undecided. Clearly, this is one area in need of further research, not only regarding people's opinions but with regard to the effects on the woman, the children, and the father. It would appear that creative solutions to this issue are also in order.

Alcohol Abuse

And finally, we wanted to determine how people felt about alcohol abuse. If such abuse is discontinued, would battering also be solved? Predictably, in view of the information given during several speeches and workshops regarding the relationship between alcohol abuse and battering, respondents disagreed (84.03%) that solving alcohol abuse would solve battering (See Table 12).

Discussion

To begin with, the authors feel that the demographic characteristics of the respondents to this survey indicate that persons who are well-educated, professionally occupied, and reasonably young are eager for some answers to this newly surfaced problem. The issues are knotty and the respondents honestly, and sometimes painfully, let us know through long narrative answers that these were not questions which could be

TABLE 11
Visitation Rights to Children

	Female (N=105)		Male (N=10)		Total (N=115)	
	N	%	N	%	N	%
"Child visitation rights should be denied the battering spouse":						
Strongly agree	18	(17.14)	1	(10)	19	(16.52)
Agree	26	(24.76)	2	(20)	28	(24.35)
Undecided	43	(40.95)	4	(40)	47	(40.87)
Disagree	14	(13.33)	–	–	14	(12.17)
Strongly disagree	4	(3.81)	3	(30)	7	(6.09)

answered through forced-choice answers but required far more insight and in-depth responses than we had allowed.

Mostly, this survey told us that we know too little. The research related throughout the earlier part of this book continually points to the conflicts, the hard questions, and the elusive answers. We believe this survey told us that there are some areas in which more needs to be done and what some of those areas might be. We considered this a pilot survey when we began; we are not sure it is even that decisive at its finish. It seems clear to us that instruments for conducting well-designed and well-controlled studies on attitudes toward battering need to be validated.

As indicated throughout this paper, there are a number of places where this survey led us to believe we might fruitfully examine the larger populations for some answers. To begin with, the small percentages of police officers (2.5%), legal personnel (5.83%), educators (5.83%), and physicians (8.33%) included in our conference participants is alarming when one realizes that these are the persons who either give or deny service to battered women. It would appear that we need a widespread effort to educate personnel in these fields. The authors decided to insert a question about violence toward animals to ascertain whether or not violence toward people

TABLE 12
Alcohol and Battering

	Female (N=109)		Male (N=10)		Total (N=119)	
	N	%	N	%	N	%
"If we could solve the problems of alcohol abuse, the problems of domestic violence would be nearly solved"·						
Strongly agree	3	(2.75)	1	(10)	4	(3.36)
Agree	6	(5.50)	1	(10)	7	(5.88)
Undecided	5	(4.59)	3	(30)	8	(6.72)
Disagree	56	(51.38)	2	(20)	58	(48.74)
Strongly disagree	39	(35.78)	3	(30)	42	(35.29)

may be displaced onto creatures of lesser power. Almost 20% of the women and 30% of the men had battered animals. Unfortunately, we do not know how to predict if these people will be inclined to inflict violence onto people. We can speculate in terms of displacement of aggression theories that those who in fact batter animals may have a higher need to inflict violence or have a lower frustration tolerance than those who do not batter animals. Further research needs to be done—perhaps in cooperation with animal protection societies, child abuse teams, and battered women shelters—to determine whether the persons who batter animals also tend to batter humans. If this is indeed the case, we might then begin a central reporting policy wherein any person reported to have battered a child, woman, or animal might be watched to determine what, or who, else they might be battering.

Maccoby and Jacklin (1974) allude to the explanation about why the women in our sample might be more fearful of battering or violence than would be expected in view of their minimal exposure to violence as children and adults:

> Girls then build up greater anxieties about aggression, and greater inhibitions against displaying it; the result is that their

aggressive impulses find expression in displaced, attenuated or disguised forms [p. 234].

Women may fear violence not because of their previous experience with it (or lack of it) but because of their realistic understanding that when compared to men, women do not have equivalent physical strength or societal power. As awareness of this becomes more entrenched through adulthood, women eventually may become fearful of what men have but they do not—physical power. Obviously, then, the fear is based not only on reality but on the realization of helplessness in a male-dominated society in a physical and symbolic sense.

The indication that fears of violence are great, even in the absence of violent experiences, lends itself to communications research. If we teach men and women to more openly accept and communicate their hostility and to learn alternative ways of expressing anger, would we simultaneously decrease the cross-sex fear of violence?

It seems obvious to the authors, given the very small number of male participants in this survey, that much more needs to be known about male experiences and attitudes toward violence. It would seem that either we had an unusually nonviolent population of males or that we had a group of males to whom it was unacceptable to express violent experiences or attitudes. At any rate, further work needs to be done with men, both regarding experiences and attitudes, and regarding formulation of possible solutions to battering.

And finally, we believe a look at priorities between battered women and children may be a necessity as funding sources for social service agencies become fewer. If it is true that men are the decision makers with regard to funding and if it is true that they consider women less important than children, then we need to begin looking seriously at how such problems might be resolved.

If would appear that this study provided us with more questions than answers, but we do believe it is a beginning in an area which has too long been unexplored.

Summary

1. Of the 120 respondents, 110 (91.6%) were women, 10 (8.3%) were men.

2. Most of the men were 24 years of age or younger; most of the women were between the ages of 25 and 34.

3. Most of the women were students; most of the men were in counseling and psychology or police work.

4. The majority of the respondents (70.8%) had either a bachelor or master's degree.

5. The largest percentage (35.03%) attended the conference because it was related to their current job.

6. Most of the respondents attended the conference to obtain information regarding battering (44.57%) and most had these expectations met.

7. Most of the participants had not experienced battering but most of the women had feared physical violence at the hands of men.

8. Most of the respondents believed that battering was due to socialization patterns (65.22%). Men did not feel that male superiority in society or male attitudes toward women or the response of the courts affect battering, while women did.

9. Most respondents believed it was important to work with batterers.

10. Both men and women stated that battering should not be considered a family affair and is in fact a public problem and that police officers view battering as a family affair.

11. The majority of the respondents stated that battering should be reported in the same way as abused children and that a protocol should be established and enforced by legal codes.

12. More women than men were in favor of denying visitation rights to the batterer.

13. Most respondents did not believe that solving alcohol abuse would solve battering.

14. Future research issues regarding battered women were suggested.

APPENDIX A

LEGAL RIGHTS OF
BATTERED WOMEN

Prepared by

The Legal Committee of
La Casa de las Madres and

The San Francisco Commission
on the Status of Women

PEOPLE WHO WORKED ON THIS HANDBOOK

Research and Writing

Lil Spitz
Liz Hendrickson
Margaret Johnson
Mary Vail
Ruth Edelstein

Editing, Support, and Encouragement

Del Martin
Jill Lippitt
Marta Ashley
Sally Potter
Sandi Blair
Shea Hester
Susan Almond

Introduction
How To Use This Handbook

This handbook was written over the past two years by a group of San Francisco law students who've worked at La Casa de las Madres (a San Francisco shelter for battered women). We wanted to make information on how to use the legal system available to battered women and women working with shelters.

We hope you can get quick answers from this handbook by reading specific sections; but we also advise you to read through the whole thing—you might find out about something that can be helpful to you.

In general, we've found it's best to take a friend with you when you deal with any part of the legal system. Especially when you're upset, someone else with you can remember to ask questions and can help present your story.

One thing our experience has shown us is that our society doesn't really think it's wrong for men to abuse, harass, intimidate or control women, and our laws and legal systems really show it. If you've tried to use the legal system to protect yourself, you've already experienced the disappointment, discouragement and even hostility that's there on every level. Until we live in a society that really respects women and all people we can expect little help or support from our institutions, including the legal system; but we're convinced we must continue to demand it.

(We want to say clearly that we don't think men are the enemy. Men are abused and degraded in this society too—especially poor, old and non-white men.)

We use the legal system because it's all we have right now. We stop short of doing things we think are totally wrong—like deporting men or committing them to mental hospitals. In the name of helping battered women, we don't want to become partners with groups trying to build more prisons, restore the death penalty or stir up racist hysteria. We try to work with the legal system to protect battered women; but we also try and stay clear about what the bigger, more long-term, picture is. We want women to be safer now, AND we want a better society for everybody in the future.

Ruth Edelstein
Liz Hendrickson

THE CRIMINAL JUSTICE SYSTEM

If your husband or boyfriend is beating, threatening or harassing you, he is committing a crime. You have the right to call the police to protect you or to arrest him. In California, there are laws which can be applied to a home violence situation. They are listed in the back of this section of the handbook and you should look at them. As important as knowing what the law says, however, is knowing how to use it. The following sections will describe how to use the police and the courts.

The Police

There are no magic tricks to getting the police to come when you need them or getting them to help you once they arrive; but it may be helpful if we outline generally what the police can do if you're in immediate danger, if you're being beaten or harassed by a man you live with, or if you're being hurt by someone you don't live with.

Calling the Police

Small towns have just one police station which people from all parts of the town go to and call when they need help. Big cities have a main police station (with offices for investigators, detectives, police complaints, jail) and smaller neighborhood stations for day-to-day business and problems. If you live in a city with neighborhood or district stations, that is where you should call or go to for help.

If you're in immediate danger when you call the police, tell them that you are in danger and need their help immediately. If the man is drunk or on drugs, if he has a gun, knife, or club, if he has hurt you before, or if you're afraid for yourself or your children, let the police know about it on the phone. Try to explain your situation clearly and quickly. It won't help to exaggerate or misstate what is happening; this will make the police suspicious of everything else you say and could make them very uncooperative.

If the police don't come in a few minutes, call them again or call the shelter in your area—they can often help get a police response by calling and saying how urgent the situation is.

When the Police Arrive

Try to talk to the officers alone. They will often separate you and the man and talk to each of you. The police don't need to know about your relationship. They DO need to know about your injuries and what has happened to you.

If you want to leave the house, the police can stay while you get together a few things for yourself and your children. If the man is the father of your children, the police don't have to let you take the children with you if the man objects; but sometimes they will. (See the section on child custody.) The police may drive you to a nearby hospital or police station or other safe place. Check with them before you leave to see if they'll give you a ride; otherwise, use the time they're there to call a friend or a cab. If you have time, get your important papers together—these might include birth certificates for your children, Medi-Cal cards, food stamp ID cards, check book, insurance policies, charge cards, deeds, social security cards, etc.

Arrest and Citizen's Arrest

If you want your attacker arrested, this can happen in several ways. If the police see the man hurting you they can arrest him. If you are hurt very badly (bleeding, broken bones), they can arrest him even though they didn't see him injure you if it looks like he did it, if you say he did it or if he admits he did it.

If the police don't see the man hurt you and you are not visibly badly injured, they can't arrest him on their own; you must ask for a citizen's arrest. To make a citizen's arrest you must tell the police:

(1) That a crime has been committed. (Do this by describing what happened.)
(2) Who your attacker was.
(3) That you want to make a citizen's arrest and that you are willing to sign a citizen's arrest card.

Once you have gone through these steps, the police officer legally must take your attacker to jail. If the officer is hesitant about cooperating with you, tell him or her that you know that you have a legal right to make a citizen's arrest under Penal Code Section 837, and that once you go through the above steps, he or she is legally obligated to take your attacker into custody for you. If all else fails, tell the officer that Penal Code Section 142 says it is a felony for a police officer to refuse to enforce the law when a crime has been committed.

You can make a citizen's arrest for either a felony or a misdemeanor.[1] Also, remember that besides assault and battery, the man can be arrested for disturbing the peace or trespassing if he doesn't live with you.

If your attacker has left the house before the police arrive, you cannot make a citizen's arrest, but you should make sure that a police report is made and file a complaint the next day with the General Works Department in San Francisco. (In other cities, go to the police and ask where to go to file a complaint.) Filing a complaint is the first step in getting an arrest warrant issued and having the man picked up by the police and either held or ordered to come to court.

Citation

If the police do not want to arrest your attacker, there is a third procedure in addition to police arrest and citizen's arrest called a "citation." A citation is like a traffic ticket—the police fill out a form that says your attacker must appear in court on a certain date. A citation is much less serious than an arrest because your attacker doesn't have to be taken away from the house in order for the police to give him a citation; the police can decide, however, to take the man away and give him a citation at the police station.

After Arrest

You must be aware that once your attacker has been arrested and taken to the police station, it is likely that he will be out again in a short period of time. If he has money for bail, he will be released on bail within a few hours; if he has no money for bail, but has friends and relatives who will vouch for him, he may be released without having to post any bail on his "own recognizance" (O.R.). To be released on O.R., he must promise to appear in court on a certain date for a formal hearing. Of course the more serious your injuries and the more serious the charges against him, the less likely it is that he will be released soon. It is important to understand that it is possible, and even likely, that your attacker will return to your home even after he has been arrested. So act fast.

If the Police Won't Help

Although there are lots of things the police CAN do to help you, they often don't do anything. They consider arrest the most serious step that can be taken and are often unwilling to do it. Particularly in situations involving domestic violence, the police are often afraid to interfere (police are injured and killed on this type of call more than any other); the police may side with the man or try to talk to him for a few minutes and then leave. If you are sure you want the man arrested, you have the right to insist that he be arrested. If the police won't help you, take down their names and badge numbers—they must give them to you. You can call the police station while the officers are still at your home and complain that they won't help you. You can also call the shelter in your area; they can sometimes talk to the police and convince them to take some action. If the police still won't do anything, use the minutes they are there to safely leave the house. If they don't arrest the man now, you may still be able to get him arrested and to press charges against him later.

The Police Report

The police report of this incident is your proof that it happened. When dealing with anyone from the DA to welfare workers, if you don't have a police report, an incident might as well have never happened. Even if you don't want to press charges or have the man arrested now, you may want to do something at a later time and you will need a police report to do anything. Remember that criminal and civil suits depend on police reports.

Just because the police come to your home or take your attacker out for a walk around the block is no guarantee that they have written a report about what happened. They don't have to write up every call that they take. You can only be sure a report is written if you see it or if the man is arrested. If the police don't write out the report at your house, arrange to go to the police station with them or the next day to make sure it gets done. Ask for the number of the police report; then you can ask for it by number; also you know they're really going to make a report if they give it a number.

If you are attacked and don't call the police, you can still make a report later. Go to the station nearest your home. Try and go within 24 hours of the incident. This deadline is set up by the police because they feel that if you wait any longer than a day to report the attack that you're probably not serious about doing anything about it. Also, it is difficult for the police to investigate an old crime.

Make sure the report is complete; if you have injuries, if the house is busted up, if the man was drunk or had a weapon, if any witnesses saw or heard him breaking in or hurting you—all of this information needs to be in the report. You can also ask the police to take pictures of your injuries or the damage to the house, or you can take pictures yourself.

Once the police report is finished, you can get a copy of it. (You have to pay for it—a few dollars.) Especially if you are leaving the area, you should get a copy of each police report—you can use them to back up your story when you need to tell people in other places what happened to you.

Other Things the Police Can Do

The police enforce the criminal law. They are also the people who enforce civil court orders because it is a crime to violate a court order. If you get a restraining order or court orders about your children or home or property and the man involved refuses to cooperate, you can call the police. (See the section on TROs for a more complete discussion of how to use police to enforce court orders.)

The police will also do things that aren't exactly enforcing the law but are part of their job of protecting you and generally keeping the peace. They will sometimes give your home special attention on their beats or escort you home from work. We've had very good luck with police going back with women to their homes to pick up personal belongings after they've left. Most police departments do this as part of their routine duties and we advise women to always have a police escort when going home for things, even if the man is not expected to be there.

The District Attorney

After dealing with the police, the next set of officials to deal with is the District Attorney's Office. They decide which cases to take to trial. You cannot go to them until you've dealt with the police and filed a police report. They depend on police investigators to give them information about a case that they use in making their decision about going to trial or not.

The D.A. is a very important person to you. Once the police investigation is finished they make decisions about prosecuting and they are the people who actually negotiate with the man's defense lawyer and the judge about charges and sentencing. Your D.A. is the person you most need to give information to about the crime. Even a good police report can't have everything in it—it may say you're hurt and going to a doctor—tell the D.A. exactly how badly you were hurt—take in pictures and describe any internal injuries. Tell the D.A. about other beatings, weapons you've been threatened with that the police didn't see, other people the man has beaten, other arrests or convictions in other cities or states for violence or related crimes like drugs or drinking. Although all this information can't be used at trial, it will give the D.A. a clearer picture of how serious the crime is so he or she will know how much to compromise or bargain.

If Your Attacker Was Arrested by the Police

When an arrest is made the District Attorney's office may draw up a complaint without you having to do anything. The complaint represents the D.A.'s decision to take a case to court. As the victim of the crime, you will be asked to come to the D.A.'s office and sign the complaint within a day or two after the arrest. Although the D.A. may draw up a complaint (press charges), he or she doesn't have to. The D.A. can decide to press charges or to drop them; so you should start calling the D.A. the day after the attack to find out what he or she is going to do about it. If you want to fight the D.A.'s decision not to press charges, follow the suggestions discussed below under citizen's arrest. If you do not go and sign the complaint, charges against your attacker will be dropped.

Citizen's Arrest

If your attacker was arrested by a citizen's arrest, you must go to the D.A.'s office at 9 A.M. the next work day and make a formal complaint. Although you have an absolute right to make a citizen's arrest, you do not have an absolute right to press charges. The D.A. will decide whether or not the man involved must go to trial.

If he or she decides that charges will not be brought against the man there is basically nothing you can do about it. You can try and argue with the D.A. Many people in the D.A.'s office feel that women are not serious about bringing charges against their husbands or boyfriends, and don't want to spend time working on those cases. Go to the D.A. within 24 hours; insist that you are serious; and call the shelter in your area to ask that they call the D.A. or go there with you; you might get them to change their minds.

If No Arrest

If your attacker was not arrested when the violence occurred, and you have decided that you want to try to have him brought before a judge, you must file a police report first and then go the the D.A.'s office and try to get them to issue a warrant for his arrest.

The D.A. will probably want to wait for the police to investigate your report before making a decision about pressing charges. In San Francisco, the police have a General Works Department (4th floor in the Hall of Justice) which handles this investigating. In other cities this investigating unit will be called something else. An officer in this department will be assigned to your case. You should learn his or her name, call to check on your case or to give any new information that comes up. When the investigation is complete, the D.A. will make a decision which you can fight in the ways outlined above if you don't like it.

Charges

The police will tell the D.A. what they arrested the man for and/or what evidence they have about what he did. The D.A. will decide whether or not to press charges against the man and what to charge him with. They are interested in getting as many convictions or guilty pleas as possible and will choose the charge according to what they can prove. If you don't like or don't understand the charges brought against the man, ask the D.A. to explain them to you. Maybe there is a good reason for the decision; the D.A. may feel that they can't prove all the things the man did or maybe they've picked a charge that doesn't sound serious to you, but really is. An example of this is felony assault with intent to do great bodily harm and attempted murder. Many men have really tried to kill a woman but are charged with assault. This is usually done because attempted murder is much harder to prove and carries a lighter sentence than assault.

Men are almost never charged with wife beating in California. A woman must be badly hurt before this charge can be used and then the punishment is less than that given for hurting a stranger as badly.

If the D.A.'s explanation of the charge doesn't make sense to you, call the shelter or women's center in your area and ask for their support in asking for a further explanation or a new decision from the D.A.

You and the D.A.

The D.A. is not your lawyer; she or he is working for the state. You are only a witness in the trial. This means that although some D.A.s may be helpful to you, others will not. It will be very helpful to you if you can get a friend or woman from a shelter to be with you throughout your dealings with the case from signing the complaint to the trial.

If you can't get clear explanations from your D.A. about the case or your role as a witness, you can get a private lawyer to help explain what is happening. A private lawyer, however, will not have any control of the criminal trial.

The Family Relations Bureau

The Family Relations Bureau is a special office within the D.A.'s office. (It may be called something else in other counties; also small counties may not have such a bureau.) It resolves family disputes by inviting the parties into the office for an informal hearing. In San Francisco, you don't have to be married to the man to use this service. The Family Relations Bureau is not court; it is just part of the D.A.'s office. They may make referrals to legal and social service agencies, but they do not prosecute crime or require your attacker to attend a hearing or take a referral if he doesn't want to. You and your attacker will receive notice of your appointment in the mail. If your attacker fails to come to the meeting, the D.A. can go ahead with pressing charges, issuing an arrest warrant, or having the man arrested.

If you think your attacker will be impressed by such a hearing or if you want to complain about your attacker but don't want to press charges, then the Family Relations Bureau may be the place to go. Also, if there has been a lapse of time since the attack or the D.A. won't prosecute for whatever reason, then this bureau can help you by documenting the incident for future use in criminal or civil actions. Do remember, though, that once there has been a hearing in Family Relations it is almost impossible for you to press charges about this same incident.

Citation Hearings

If your attacker was cited by the police, or if the D.A. thinks that he did not commit a very serious crime, a citation hearing will be called at which your attacker will be told the charges against him and will be allowed to answer them. A hearing officer will decide whether or not a trial will be held. It is likely that the charges against the man will be dropped at the citation hearing. As the victim of the crime, you will have to be present to describe what happened. Citation hearings are basically the same as hearings with the Family Relations Bureau and are conducted by the same people.

Even though citations usually don't involve trial and jail, they can be effective against some men who don't want trouble with the law and will take seriously a warning to leave you alone. This hearing may force him to see that what he is doing is against the law.

The Court

Most criminal cases are not tried in court. They are usually settled prior to the trial. Going through a trial takes a lot of time and money and everybody, from the police to the judge, tries to settle things as early in the process as possible. Whether or not your case does go to court, this section will help you deal with what will happen if you become a witness and will also explain what's happening at different stages of the court process.

Arraignment

An arraignment is a hearing before a judge. This is the first court appearance after a person is charged with a crime. At the arraignment your attacker will be told what the charges against him are and what his constitutional rights are. These include the right to a trial by jury, to have an attorney, to have the court appoint an attorney if he can't afford one and the right to plead guilty or not guilty to the charges.

If the man is charged with a misdemeanor, he will be arraigned the day after his arrest. If he is charged with a felony, he will be arraigned within two days after the complaint is filed by the D.A. The arraignment will be held in Municipal Court. You don't have to go, but you can go. Bail in misdemeanor cases is never more than $500, which most people can raise. If you attend the arraignment in either a misdemeanor or a felony case, you can ask the D.A. and judge to make staying away from you a condition of bail. This works just like a TRO—if the man does something the court order says he shouldn't do, his bail is revoked and he goes to jail until his trial. You can talk to the D.A. about this before the arraignment, but if you actually go you can make a good case to the judge and also give him or her a complete picture of what you need; for example, staying away from the neighborhood, the babysitters, the house, your job, etc. After the arraignment you can ask the D.A. to ask the judge for a minute order which is like the order you get in a TRO. This order (like the TRO) is what you show to the police if the man violates the conditions of his bail.

If you don't go to court, you can call the court to find out what happened at any of these hearings from the arraignment to sentencing. The hearings are a public record. All you need to get the information is the man's name. The first time you call they will tell you his case number. Using the case number usually makes things easier.

Preliminary Hearing (For Felony Cases Only)

After the arraignment in a felony case, your attacker has a right to a preliminary hearing. At this hearing, a Municipal Court Judge decides whether or not there is enough evidence to take the case to trial. The D.A. would usually make sure this is true before going this far.

You are required to testify at the preliminary hearing and give your story. You will first be sworn in as a witness and then questioned by the D.A. Your attacker's attorney will cross-examine you. The D.A. should help you prepare to testify by meeting with you before the hearing. If he or she doesn't, you should call and ask to meet. You will be subpoenaed as a witness and the subpoena will usually have written on it a request for you to come in an hour before your court time to talk with the D.A.

If the judge rules that there is enough evidence in your case, then the case will be sent to Superior Court to be arraigned. It will be about three weeks before this arraignment and then 60 days before a trial.

Pre-trial Proceedings

There are various pre-trial motions that can be filed by the attorneys. These and other matters are discussed at the pre-trial hearing. This hearing is before the Superior Court judge who will hear the case if it comes to trial. You may be required to come to this hearing and to testify, but usually you will not.

Misdemeanor Plea Bargaining: The D.A. and your attacker's attorney will plea bargain; plea bargaining is when the D.A. lowers the charge against your attacker if your attacker will plead guilty right away instead of having a trial. Often, the sentence for your attacker will be discussed when they are plea bargaining. At the pre-trial hearing, your attacker then will plead guilty or not guilty to the charges, whether or not he has plea bargained.

Felony Plea Bargaining: In San Francisco, the D.A. does not usually plea bargain in felony cases. This means that your attacker will be tried on the original charges and nothing less. There may still be a discussion with the judge at the pre-trial hearing of the sentence and a chance for the man to plead guilty. Again, it is important that the D.A. knows your whole story so he or she will know whether or not to agree to a lower charge. In other counties felonies may be plea bargained and the charges lowered.

The Trial

Many cases don't get as far as a trial because the defendant (your attacker) pleads guilty or the charges are dropped. If your case does go to trial, this is where all the evidence on both sides is heard and a decision is made by a jury. You will have to testify at the trial, but you don't have to be there on days when you aren't testifying. Most of the time you CAN'T be in the courtroom while other witnesses are testifying and they can't be there while you are. You have to wait in the hall outside. During these times, it is very helpful to have a friend with you since your attacker's family and friends may be walking in and out of the courtroom, glaring at you or harassing you. If they threaten or bother you, tell the D.A. He or she can arrange for you to have an escort home and even police protection if you are in serious danger. Anyone not testifying at the trial can stay in the courtroom and watch the whole thing.

As you can see, the court process can take weeks or months. The man who attacked you may be out on the streets all this time. Even if he is in jail his friends or family may threaten you. If you've decided to leave the area for your safety, talk to the D.A. about this too. They have money to use to transport witnesses from other cities or even other states—you don't have to stay in town until the whole court process is over. San Francisco has a program called the Victim/ Witness Assistance Program to help people with these arrangements.

You should also think about protecting your safety in your new location. The D.A. has some discretion about giving the defense lawyer your new address. In general, they are supposed to give out your new address to the defense. It is important to keep in touch with the D.A. during this time and to give them a way to reach you when they need you; but if you are in danger and the D.A. doesn't seem to understand this, you might want to give the D.A. a relative's or friend's phone number and then tell them to contact you when the D.A. calls. This way the trial can go on and you can be safe.

Sentencing

After your attacker has been found guilty at trial or has pled guilty, a date will be set for sentencing. This should be within a few weeks. During this time, your attacker will probably be under investigation by the adult probation department. This investigation is to find out about the man's life so that the probation department can make a recommendation to the judge about what to do with him. The victim (you) is usually contacted by the probation officer to come in and talk. If you have feelings or opinions about what should happen to your attacker, now is the time to talk. If you are not contacted by the probation department, you should call them and make an appointment.

Here is a list of some things you might want to talk to the probation officer about: Any drug or alcohol problems of the man, what you know about his violence like other times he was violent with you, other times the man was involved with the police in other states or countries.

After this investigation, the probation officer makes a recommendation to the court about the sentence. The court will usually follow this recommendation although they don't have to. If there was a plea bargain, the sentence could be a part of the deal and the P.O.'s recommendation will have no effect on the sentence.

At the sentencing hearing the judge makes the final decision based on the crime and the man's previous offenses and anything else he or she thinks is important. It could be a jail term, a prison term, probation or a combination of these and other programs like drug or alcohol treatment programs. You can call the court or the D.A. to find out what the sentence is.

If You Lose the Trial

You probably won't lose the trial—if you make it past the police, investigators, and district attorney to court, you'll probably win. D.A.s don't want to spend time on cases that accomplish nothing, so they try and only take winners.

Still, you might lose. In almost two years at La Casa, we've only seen this happen once—the jury believed the man's story more than the woman's. After going through all the hassles of pressing charges and going to trial, it is pretty upsetting to wind up with nothing. Take advantage of friends and support groups to get you through this time. ALSO, remember that you have accomplished something because you've stood up to someone who was making your life miserable and you've made it easier for women coming after you.

If you lose the trial, you can't use the D.A. and the courts again for this incident; although you can go through it all again if the man attacks you again.

If you need protection from the man, you can use civil means to get help—a restraining order for instance—without having to wait for him to hurt you again.

Parole and Probation

People who have already spent time in prison but who have time left to serve on their sentences are on parole and report to the California Adult Authority. Each person has a parole agent. The agent makes reports and recommendations to the Adult Authority.

If you are being hurt or bothered by a man on parole, find out who his parole agent is and go talk to him. To find out the name of the parole agent, call the nearest Adult Authority office. In big cities look in the phone book under California State—Corrections Department—Adult Authority and Parole. If you don't live near an office, call or write the office in Sacramento: California Department of Corrections, Parole and Community Services, 714 P Street, Sacramento, 914-445-6532 or 914-445-9417 nights and weekends.

Write a letter detailing what has happened to you and what you are afraid of. Send copies of police reports or restraining orders and keep copies of everything you send.

Parole officers vary—some are very sympathetic, some are very discouraging. They may honestly not be able to help you or they may not want to. If you send everything in writing to go into the man's file, another agent may decide to use it later; so keep trying. If you feel you have a good case that isn't getting attention, you can go to the Supervisor of the Parole Office and then to the County Supervisor.

Hearings are held periodically (once or twice a year) to review how a person on parole is doing. Also, hearings are held when the board is considering changing a person's status (letting them off parole or sending them back to prison). You may be asked to attend a hearing. The Board cannot subpoena you like a court, so it can't punish you if you refuse to go. But, unlike court, you cannot go to the hearing unless they invite you. You may wish to watch or speak but they don't have to let you in.

Beating or harassing a woman is not necessarily a reason the Parole Board will use to send a man back to prison. However, some parole agents realize that a man is heading for trouble with the police if he doesn't change his behavior. Sometimes if the agent warns the man of this, the man might stop. Also, violation of a restraining order is a violation of parole and could result in action by the Adult Authority. Therefore, men on parole stand more to lose than others and may be more impressed by restraining orders.

When dealing with the Adult Authority, you should try and keep a cautious attitude, just like dealing with any part of the legal system. Although some man on parole is terrorizing you and your family, if he doesn't violate a law, his harassment of you may not even be considered or discussed by the Adult Authority. It is likely that you would be refused a chance to tell your story to the Board. That doesn't mean that you shouldn't try to get help from them; it just means that you should be careful not to get your hopes up.

PROBATION is a system somewhat like parole, but different. People are put on probation by the court instead of being put in jail. They may be ordered to report to the court or to the Adult Probation Department. If they go to Adult Probation, they will have a probation officer, like a parole agent, who you can contact if you're having problems with the man. If they go to court, they will not have a probation officer. Actions on cases in this category are taken by the D.A.'s office.

You can approach a man on probation just like a man on parole: Talk to his P.O., send copies of police reports and restraining orders. If the man is on probation in another county, the authorities in that county will not automatically be notified of his actions in other parts of the state. It is important that you tell them. Also, some probation includes not leaving the area. If a man is travelling some distance to harass you, his P.O. may be able to help control him.

Like a parole agent, a probation officer may call the man in and talk with him about not harassing you. If the man is arrested, or a police report about an incident is filed, you have the best chance of getting help from the P.O. Even without either of these things, however, the P.O. may be able to assist you by making a motion to review probation on the basis of your statements. If he or she does, a court hearing would take place, but the judge would make the final decision. Three things may happen as a result of this hearing:

(1) The man may be reprimanded or warned. A record of this will be put in his file and referred to if he's called in again.

(2) His probation may be modified. It could be extended; he could be required to report to the P.O. more often; the court could order him not to bother you.

(3) His probation could be revoked, which means he would go to jail for the rest of his original sentence.

If the man is on probation for traffic offenses, his actions toward you may not be seen as related to his probation, even if he's arrested. If the traffic probation is for use of drugs or alcohol, however, they could be related and you should contact the P.O.

If the man you are afraid of is in prison, you can call the Sacramento numbers listed above; ask for the records department and find out when the man will be released from prison and in what area he will be released.

Other groups which help families of prisoners and ex-prisoners are listed in the resource list. Some offer support to families while the man is in prison; and some offer counselling to help ex-prisoners readjust to their families after getting out.

Other Ways of Dealing with Harassment

This section is especially for women who don't live with a man who is harassing them. Many women are harassed by ex-husbands and boyfriends or even by men they've met but never had a relationship with. These men come to their homes or jobs and threaten and harass them. Often they use the telephone to bother the woman; sometimes they threaten or kidnap the woman's children.

Dealing with this kind of abuse is different and in some ways harder than dealing with someone you live with or know well. Although this type of harassment has received less publicity than wife beating, it is just as serious. Women have been hurt and terrorized by men they don't live with or have never lived with and barely know.

Because this type of harassment is talked about less than violence in the home, public agencies are less sympathetic to its victims. Police don't believe you don't really know the man or refuse to arrest an ex-husband or former boyfriend for trespassing or breaking into your home, especially if they once lived with you.

The Civil Section of the handbook talks about some things you can do if either you live with the man who is harassing you or if you don't. Besides those and the things we've already discussed, the ideas in this section are some things we've tried that might help.

Support from Your Neighbors: Many women who call us don't know their neighbors and don't feel they can call on them for help and support. If someone is breaking into your home, your neighbors' support can be very helpful. Talk to them a little about your situation. Describe the man and his car to them. Ask them to write down descriptions and license plate numbers of cars that they see at your house at strange times of the night. Ask them to be alert to loud noises or gun shots if you're expecting that. Witnesses to these kinds of crimes can make a real difference in how the police treat you. Also, sympathetic neighbors can help you when and if you're in danger. Certainly you may get nowhere in talking to people—many people won't want to get involved, but it's worth a try.

Your Job: Men often harass women at their jobs—sometimes by calling or coming by, sometimes by following them home from work and attacking them there or on the way. If you can get the support of the people you work with, they can help you in the same ways your neighbors can. Your employer or co-workers can also call the police and have the man arrested for trespassing or disturbing the peace if he comes to your work.

The police may or may not be helpful to you at your job or on your way home. They may escort you home or ask the man to leave if he's hanging around your work. They may, unfortunately, tell you that there's nothing they can do until the man hurts you. Check the section on arrest and citizen's arrest; it applies here too.

Restraining Orders: Read the section on TROs. You don't need to be married to a person to get a restraining order against him. You DO need to be living with him, if you're not married to him. If you're married, you don't need to file for a divorce to get a restraining order, though you can get a TRO with a divorce.

Prevention/Precautions: Choose your home carefully. If you've been harassed by someone who may continue to bother you, you might consider living with other people rather than by yourself. Pick a neighborhood where you already have friends who can help you if there's trouble.

Be careful about who you give your home or work address to. If you move away from a husband or boyfriend who has acted jealous and possessive before, think twice before giving him your new address. Meet him somewhere else when you see him. If you have children, read the section on child custody.

If a man has beaten or harassed you at least make a police report. He is more likely to become more abusive than less and these reports can back up your claims later. Read the sections on arrest and dealing with the district attorney. Also, if the man is on parole or probation, read that section.

If the man harassing you is someone you used to live with or be married to, or is the father of your children, read the sections on divorce, especially the parts about temporary orders, getting the man out of the house and TROs.

The Man's Work: Many companies have special programs to help their workers with drinking, drugs, and other problems. We've had a little luck in dealing with the programs. If you know where the man works, call there or ask a shelter or rape worker to call.

Men's Groups: One other source of help that's just starting to become available are men's groups. The East Bay and San Francisco both have groups of men willing to talk to men who rape or batter women. This may be especially helpful to women who are being harassed by men and can't or don't want to get help from the police. Rape groups or battered women's groups are usually in contact with these men's groups.

See also the Civil Section on Getting the Man out of the House.

California Criminal Laws

Assault: Being threatened with physical violence is a crime. You don't have to be hurt to charge your attacker with assault; but you have to be able to prove that you were threatened and that the man had the ability to hurt you *at that time.* (Penal Code Sections 240 & 241)

Battery: This crime has been committed when any force or violence has occurred against you. You don't have to be seriously hurt to charge someone with battery. Punishment for this crime depends on how seriously you have been hurt. (Penal Code Sections 242 & 243)

Assault with a Deadly Weapon: The law prohibits any attack on a person with a deadly weapon (gun, knife, lead pipe, etc.) or when the force of the attack is "likely to produce great bodily injury." Like in assault, the attack or the threat of attack is illegal; you don't need to be hurt by your attacker. (Penal Code Sections 244 & 245)

Wife Beating: Wife beating is a separate crime that applies only to violence by a husband against his wife. To bring a charge of wife beating, there must be bodily injury that results in a "traumatic condition." The words traumatic condition apply only when there is serious physical injury to the wife (broken bones, internal bleeding, serious wounds, etc.). Of all the crimes listed, wife beating is the most difficult to prove. (Penal Code Section 273(d))

If you are not married, or are legally separated or divorced and are not legally sharing a home or apartment with the man who beats or threatens you, there are two additional crimes that can be charged:

Burglary: If any person enters your home or apartment illegally, with the intent to commit any felony,[2] he is committing a burglary. Therefore, if a man enters your home without permission and with the intention of seriously hurting you, he is committing a crime. (Penal Code Section 459)

Trespass: If any person enters your home or apartment without your permission, he is guilty of trespass. There does not have to be any violence or threat of violence to charge someone with this crime. (Penal Code Section 602.5)

Sentencing: As of July 1, 1977, a new sentencing law was passed in California which says that there are three different sentences for each crime which depend on how serious the crime is and on the person's past record. For most crimes listed in this handbook, the sentence can be 2, 3, or 4 years in state prison. (This is for felony crimes only.) The middle number (3 years) is the usual sentence. If the person has little or no record and the circumstances of the crime are not that serious, they may be given a two-year sentence. If the circumstances of the crime are very serious and the person has a long record, they can be given four years.

CIVIL LAW

Divorce and Legal Separation

It's easy for people to say that if your husband beats you, you should get a divorce. While it's true that a man has no right to hit a woman, many of us are emotionally and economically tied to our husbands, and to think about something as permanent as a divorce can be pretty scary.

We've come to see that divorce can have strategic value just like calling the police or getting a restraining order. Maybe you're clear that you want to end your marriage and get a divorce; maybe you want some time away from your husband to sort things out; maybe you think filing for a divorce will shake him up and make him realize you won't stay unless he changes. It could be that when you take this step it's the first time you've been able to do anything about being beaten. Your husband is then faced with your power, your lawyer and the court, all at once, and he may be forced to look at what's happening for the first time.

The same papers are filed and the same hearings held for separations as for divorces (called dissolutions in California.) They aren't any easier or cheaper. If you don't want a divorce for religious or other reasons, you might want a separation. In either case, if you change your mind before the final decree is made (at the end of six months) you can just drop the whole thing. Either a separation or divorce becomes final at the end of six months.

Both separation and divorce offer you certain protections. Although some couples just separate without going to court and getting an official divorce or separation agreement, you might want some of the protections they include.

If you have children or property the court will make official whatever arrangements you and your husband decide on; or, if you can't agree, will hold hearings and make decisions. These court orders you may enforce by going back to court or by calling the police. Without them you really can't do anything if your husband takes the children or spends your money or takes or sells your property. Even if you don't want a divorce, you may want an official statement of how things will be while you're separated.

If you have no children, not much property and do not expect problems in working out a divorce or separation agreement with your husband, you may fill out and file your own divorce papers without a lawyer, saving yourself attorney's fees. If you are poor, such as on welfare, you may get the court filing fees waived; talk to the court clerk when you file the papers. Several Bay Area groups offer workshops on doing your own divorce; check the resource list. If you have any questions about whether or not you should do your own divorce, consult with a lawyer. See the section on choosing a lawyer also.

Legal Myths about Divorce and the Battered Wife

No. 1. "My husband says he won't give me a divorce."
In California, since 1970, you can get a "no-fault" divorce. This means:

—that either party can file for divorce
—you don't need to have any special reason to get a divorce, that you don't get along and want to end the marriage is enough
—as long as you don't make up with your husband and you show up in court, the divorce will go through whether your husband likes it or not.

The only requirements for a California divorce are:

(1) either person must be a resident of California for at least six months before filing for divorce;
(2) that person must be a resident of the county where the divorce is filed for at least three months before filing;
(3) the couple has "irreconcilable differences"—this means there are problems you and your husband can't work out;
(4) a filing fee of about $50.00 (if you are on welfare or can show you are poor the fee will be waived).

Your husband does have the right to ask for marriage counseling before going ahead with the divorce, and you have to participate, if the judge agrees. These counseling sessions won't hold up the final divorce or your court hearings and decisions on temporary support, child custody, etc.

No. 2. "If I leave my husband and then try to get a divorce, I'll be charged with desertion and won't get anything."
Not true.

First of all, no one will charge you with desertion when you file for divorce because of the no-fault divorce laws in California.

Second, California is a "community property" state. That means that whatever property was gathered while you were married and living in California is to be divided equally between you and your husband when the marriage ends. Even property in his name alone is considered community property if it was bought or given to you during the marriage. Also, if your husband tries to fight the property division, he can only bring up evidence having to do with the property, and not about your leaving the home.

No. 3. "If I leave my husband, I won't be able to keep my children."

If you and your husband can't agree about who the children should live with, the issue is determined by the judge, and is based on the best interests of the children. According to the law, both parents have equal right to the custody of the children until it is proven that one parent is better able to take care of them. If you've been taking care of the children all along, you have a good chance of getting custody.

When you go to trial for your divorce and your husband is fighting over the custody of the children, you and your lawyer will have to prove that you would be the best person to take care of them. (For more information see the Child Custody section.)

No. 4. "My husband says he'll cut me off without a nickel if I divorce him."

Your rights to the property purchased by you and your husband are outlined in No. 2. Ongoing cash support from him is more difficult to get and collect.

If you and your husband have children, and you are given custody of them he will be ordered to make child support payments for their benefit. The amount of the payments will depend on your need for the money, and his ability to pay.

Alimony (spousal support) is *not* easy to get in California anymore. More often than not, you will be expected to get a job to support yourself with some help for the children from your husband.

You may be able to get temporary spousal support for the length of time the court thinks it will take you to find a job, but the court will usually allow long-term alimony only when the marriage has gone on for over twenty years, or where the women is sick and can't work or has a baby she has to take care of.

Of course, your husband can make it difficult for you to get the support money he owes you. More men don't pay court-ordered support than do.

No. 5. "I can't afford a lawyer to fight my husband in court, so I'm going to settle with whatever he'll give me."

There's no reason for a woman to accept her husband's terms for a divorce in a state with laws like California. No-fault divorce is designed to prevent this and groups exist to help poor people get divorces.

If you don't have much money, go to legal aid. All Bay Area legal aid societies handle divorces. If you don't qualify for legal aid but don't have cash to pay a lawyer, you can sometimes get someone to represent you for a small amount now with the rest paid in monthly installments or when the divorce is final. If you and your husband own a home or other property, your attorney can be paid when that property is divided and sold—sometimes the court will order the lawyers' fees to come out of your husband's money, if he has a better job than you.

Although it's a hassle, don't give up without a fight.

No. 6. "I don't care about the house and the money; I don't ever want to see him again. He can have everything."

You probably shouldn't make this decision until you've talked to a lawyer. Maybe there's really not enough property to make it worth the trouble, but maybe you'll decide to take a car or furniture.

Most of us feel like this for a while after leaving an abusive marriage. Unless you're worried that your husband will sell or run off with all the property and money, you can wait until you feel up to it to file for a divorce and deal with all this.

Your lawyer can deal with a lot of the negotiations with your husband's lawyer and keep the contact between the two of you to a minimum. Remember that you can file for a divorce and receive your share of the community property even after you've been separated for years; though there's not much you can do if your husband spends and sells it all before then.

Temporary Orders and Court Hearings

Emergency Orders

The law allows for some protections in connection with a divorce or separation through emergency orders from the court. When you file your papers for the divorce, you can ask the court at that time for temporary orders not only against your husband hitting or harassing you but also forbidding him to destroy any of the community property and ordering him out of the family home.

These orders are issued "ex parte" (with only one party telling their side of the story) right away when you file your papers. Orders forbidding your husband to hurt or bother you, giving you temporary custody of the children (if they're already with you), and forbidding either of you to spend or destroy the community property are pretty routine. Getting your husband ordered out of the house or getting custody of the children if they're with your husband is more difficult without having a hearing first; but you have a good chance if your husband has been violent to you or the children.

If the judge won't agree now to something you're asking for, you can file your request and the judge will decide after hearing both your sides at the OSC hearing.

Order to Show Cause Hearing (OSC)

About three weeks after your divorce petition and your temporary orders are filed and your husband is given (served) a copy of the papers, there will be an OSC hearing, if you request one. It will deal with the protections you asked for earlier, whether or not they were given to you.

At the OSC hearing, your husband will have to prove to the judge that you should not be given all the things you asked for. He may want to argue all of the issues, a few of them or none of them. You and your lawyer will work out exactly what kinds of proof will be necessary when you go to court to support your request. You will be asked to testify at the hearing to support your request and your lawyer will be able to explain to you what that will be like.

The temporary orders, as determined at the OSC hearing, will stay in effect until the interlocutory (final) trial. The interlocutory judgment will be based either on an agreement between you and your husband or the court's decisions regarding property, child custody, support money and restraining orders if you and your husband can't agree. Sometimes the courts are crowded and you have to return to court for another OSC hearing before the interlocutory trail.

Although the interlocutory judgment is "final" it can be changed later if your situation changes. For instance, if you or your husband change jobs, the amount you should each pay for supporting your children may change.

Getting the Man Out of the House

Living together while getting a divorce can be a pretty strained arrangement and you're probably moved out already. Especially if you have children, however, you may want to stay in your home and have your husband stay somewhere else while you get divorced. If your husband won't agree to leave you can ask the court to include this in its temporary orders. Many lawyers never ask and so don't get men ordered out of their homes. We've had pretty good luck in this, but you should know that the judge doesn't *have* to order him out.

Once the judge orders him out, getting it to happen may still be hard. The judge usually gives the man a certain number of days to move out. If he's not out, you can go back to court and/or call the police.

Getting the support of the police can be very difficult. Police would usually rather escort the woman and children out of the home than the man. This is one of the times you most need the support of your friends and women from a shelter group. If you're expecting trouble, talk to the police before the man's deadline about what you want from them and what they're willing to do. This will give you time to talk with your lawyer and friends and to get their help in getting police support. It's hard to do all this calm talking and planning in the middle of trying to throw the man out.

Part of the court orders should be a warning to both you and your husband not to remove or destroy the community property. If you expect trouble, talk to your lawyer about how to protect your things—get a clear agreement about what he can take and what he has to leave. Remember, though, that if he violates the court order he may get in trouble with the judge or it may affect his share of the property settlement, but you won't get your things back. You might want to store things in the meantime. (This includes money.)

Once he's out, you may have trouble keeping him out. Change the locks right away. Even though he once lived there and your divorce or separation isn't final, you can call the police if he tries to break in or comes around bothering you. This is just a matter of enforcing a TRO, so you should look at that section. Remember that you're in a hard position with the police—they have a hard time throwing a man out of his house—so don't make it more confusing for them by sometimes letting him in. If you don't want him there keep that clear by not letting him in.

Leaving the State or Country

Many battered women want to leave the state or country with their children before getting a divorce. Under the law, it is all right to leave with your children especially if divorce or custody proceedings haven't started yet. You can decide to leave California and go to another state before starting your divorce. All this means is that you will have to establish residency in the new state before you start divorce proceedings. (Usually the residency requirements in most states are between a few months and a year.) Before deciding to move out of California, check the laws in the state you're moving to. Few states have divorce laws as simple and liberal as California. You may hurt yourself by moving.

If your husband starts divorce or custody proceedings in California after you've left, he and his lawyer will have to find you and serve you with the necessary papers. Your husband may be able to get a divorce in California without you being here; he may also get custody of the children without you being here, but the court will have to find you to do anything about it. So if you decide to leave, it is usually a good idea not to let him or his family know where you are.

If you leave when the divorce has already started and if the court grants custody or visitation rights to your husband, you may be violating a court order by leaving. This means that if your husband or the court finds you, you could be held in contempt of court for leaving and fined money or put in jail until you comply with the court order. If you leave the country and don't return, American courts can do nothing to you.

If you leave the state, it is usually best to try to start divorce and custody proceedings in your new state as soon as possible. This means that your husband will be served with the papers in California. He might then decide to come to your new state and ask for custody of the children or visitation rights. (He might also just come to harass you.) In any case, he will have to come to you to argue with the court or to see the children.

If you get a divorce in California and are granted custody of your children, you don't have to stay in the state just so your ex-husband can easily visit the children. Unless your divorce orders specifically say that the children can't be removed from the state you're not doing anything wrong by leaving. Your husband may go back to court and complain, however, and you should have a good reason (a job, relatives) for moving BESIDES getting away from him.

Child Custody

Whether or not you are married, either you or the father of your children may have custody of them until a court makes a custody order. This means that you can take the children with you when you leave—it's not against the law—but their father can take them back or can refuse to let you take them—they're not more yours than his. The police will sometimes decide on the spot that a child belongs with the mother, especially if the child is very young; but you can never predict for sure that this will happen.

If you can't take your children with you when you first leave you won't automatically be judged a negligent mother and denied custody of them later. You can go back for them when it's safe or you can ask the court for custody of them, explaining that you were prevented from taking them before. However, you are in a much better position to fight for custody if you've taken the children with you.

If you're concerned about the welfare of your children you can call the Child Protective Services in your county. They will investigate and remove the children if they're in danger. This should only be done as a last, drastic step, however, since these are the people who can place children in foster homes, etc.; and once they take the children from their father they may not give them to you.

If you're getting a divorce you can get temporary custody as part of your temporary orders. Temporary visitation arrangements can also be set up. Explain to your lawyer that it's important to get these quickly.

While you're separated from their father but before you get a court decision about custody you don't have to let the children be seen by your husband or boyfriend. It actually may be dangerous for him to see them during this time; you'll probably be able to judge that, based on your experience with the man. Men sometimes use children to upset their mother or to tell where the woman is staying. Until you have a court order giving you custody and detailing when and how the man is to visit you have no remedy if he takes the kids and runs. Even if you have filed for divorce you should wait for your temporary orders if you have any reason to worry. Then at least you have something to use should the father try and take the children. His divorce lawyer (and sometimes his defense lawyer in criminal cases!) will call you and ask for visitation but you can and probably should refuse (if you have reason to worry) until he gets a court order.

If you're not married to the children's father you can still go to court and settle issues of paternity, custody and visitation.

In deciding custody in California the court no longer assumes that the mother is the best parent for a child to live with. If the child is an infant the mother usually will get custody, but otherwise the person best for the child is supposed to be awarded custody. Work with your lawyer in proving that the children will be best off with you—including bringing up information about their father and ways he may be unable to care for them. Unfortunately the fact that a man has beaten the children's mother will not automatically make him unable to care for them in the court's opinion, and he could be awarded custody.

As part of the decision-making process the court will use the social service agencies of the county. You, the children and their father will be interviewed by a social worker who will then make a recommendation to the judge. If you are poor or out of work you will not be denied custody because of that; the court doesn't look at how much money you have to support the children but at the care, love, and attention you give them.

Once the court makes a final decision you or your husband can go back to court at any time until your youngest child is 18 and try and have the custody arrangements modified or changed. You should be prepared for this and also should realize that if you are denied custody at first you can go back and fight the decision again, especially if your situation changes.

Enforcing the Custody Order

Once you get custody you can go back to court or call the police if the man doesn't honor the order. Like a TRO, a custody order isn't magic, though. Even though he doesn't have legal custody, a father is considered a suitable person to have a child and police usually don't get too upset if a parent is late returning a child from a visit or even steals the child and heads out of town.

Like a TRO, a custody order can be enforced either by calling the police or by going back to court.

Visitation

Only in very extreme cases, when a parent has abused a child, will the court refuse to allow some visitation for the parent not awarded custody. Standard in this area is two weekends a month and some time in the summer.

These visits can be very tense and even dangerous for battered women. You can work out with your lawyer some guidelines to protect you, which the court can adopt. These might include visits to be held at some third person's house, so you don't have to give your new address to the man, and visits to be in the presence of a third party to prevent the abuse or abduction of the children. These provisions will help prevent your being harassed by the man; however, our experience is that children are usually charmed, tricked, or intimidated into giving their father their address and you should think about what to do if that happens.

Children Taken Out of the Country

If you're worried about the children being taken out of the country by their father, you can write the U.S. Passport Office (William B. Wharton, Chief, Legal Division, Passport Office, 1425 K Street NW, Washington, D.C. 20005) and give them the names, birth dates, and descriptions of your children and their father. Also send them a certified copy of your custody order and a restraining order forbidding the children to be taken out of the country. Include your home and work address and phone number.

If their father applies for a passport for your children, the Passport Office will notify you. If they have on file a court order forbidding the removal of the children from the country or if you send such an order before the date they set to leave, their passport application will be denied. Once a passport has been issued, however, they will not revoke it. They will send you the child's address as listed on the passport and they will help you locate your child in another country and obtain duplicate passports for them in order to bring them home. You can't just get a court order in the U.S. and send it to another country and expect officials there to send your children back. You or a friend with your power of attorney (authorized to act for you) must go get your children.

The above applies to children who are U.S. citizens only. If your children are citizens of another country or have dual citizenship in the U.S. and another country, you should contact the Passport Office but there is little you can do.

Choosing a Lawyer

Although getting a divorce can be fairly simple, often it is not and we advise that most women find a good lawyer who will be able to present your case in the best way possible. When looking for a lawyer it is important to keep a few things in mind.

1. You don't need to know exactly what you want before talking to a lawyer. It is the lawyer's job to help you figure out what is the best strategy for you; and although you have the final word on how to handle your case, you might want some information and guidance before deciding.

2. A good lawyer is a person who knows the law that applies to you and very importantly, is a person who sympathizes with you and will give you support and encouragement. Such people do exist, so don't settle for less.

3. If you have special problems, make sure that your lawyer is an expert in that area. For instance, women with immigration problems should see a lawyer who has a lot of experience in that area. A good divorce lawyer is not necessarily a good immigration lawyer.

4. A good divorce lawyer does not necessarily cost a lot of money. Women without money can use legal aid lawyers. Women who don't qualify for legal aid can find lawyers who are willing to wait for most of their money until after your case is settled. Some lawyers will accept payment in monthly installments or will ask the court to order your husband to pay the attorney if he has more money.

5. Trust your lawyer. Your secrets are safe with him or her. By law, your lawyer can't be forced to tell anyone anything about your case. Once you've picked someone you feel good about, tell him or her everything about your case. Even if you think some things make you sound bad, tell your lawyer so he or she will have time to think about them and prepare your case well.

Checklist for Going to See Your Divorce Lawyer

Once you find a lawyer who supports you and whom you can trust, she or he will help you make decisions about your divorce and will tell you what information is needed to back up your requests.

Often, however, you will have short appointments with your lawyer and won't have time to thoroughly discuss every aspect of your case. For battered women especially this can cause a lot of confusion—documents you need may be at home with your husband or stored at a friend's house, or questions you meant to ask your lawyer are forgotten in the bustle of the office.

This checklist is just an outline of what you might need to help you prepare to see your lawyer. You should add to it yourself and redo it after talking with your lawyer. Use it to help yourself identify what information you need to start looking for and what questions you need to make sure and talk to your lawyer about:

Information to collect:

—when and where you were married;
—when you moved to California;
—addresses for your husband (work, home, relatives);
—what you and your husband own (cars, bank accounts, home property, stocks, jewelry, insurance policies, pension plans, things in other states—get together all the papers that go with these items);
—what you and your husband owe (charge accounts, loans, mortgages, medical and other bills);
—birth certificates for your children;
—social security card numbers for you and your husband.

What you need now:

—husband out of the house;
—custody of the children;
—restraining order;
—support money;
—protection for your property.

Long-term questions:

—Who will stay in the house?
—Who will the children be with permanently?
—Visitation arrangements—Is a third party needed or a neutral place?
—Support money for you and the children.
—Protection from your husband—restraining order.

Restraining Orders

Should You Get One?

We get many questions about TROs. In the past we haven't recommended them because they could be difficult, sometimes impossible to get and often weren't enforced and were therefore worthless. New laws and procedures for TROs have made them easier to get and enforce; so that we now think that a TRO, when used within an overall strategy, can be very effective. It's just important that you be realistic about what you're getting so you're not disappointed later.

A TRO is still not a magic answer. It doesn't give you any new protection—it's already against the law to hit and harass people—and you must rely on the same people to enforce a TRO as you do to enforce other laws—the police and the courts. The worst thing about people's attitudes toward TROs is the miracle cure reputation they have. Many women have spent a lot of time and energy getting a TRO, thinking it would quickly solve all their problems. When it didn't do that they ended up more discouraged than when they started.

Questions to think about before getting a TRO are the same ones you should ask yourself whenever you use the legal system. Don't let them scare you out of getting one; just use them to prepare yourself for doing what you have to do to enforce the TRO:

—What will the man think about it?
—Will he be scared by it and obey it?
—Will he be angered and harass you more?
—Will he be scared by the mere threat of a TRO?
—Will you have to take him back to court a few times before he's impressed?
—Will he do as he pleases and smooth talk the police and judge into not believing you?

If you decide to get a TRO, pay close attention to what it involves; you are the key person in enforcing it.

How to Get a Restraining Order

If you go to civil court in any action against the man harassing you (divorce, paternity suit) you can get, as part of that action, a Temporary Restraining Order. If you bring criminal charges against the man, you can get his leaving you alone made a condition of his bail. (See arraignment in the Criminal section.) Now, in California, you can also get a restraining order by itself, without going to court about anything else. Under this new law, if you're married you don't have to file for a divorce; if you're not married you can get a TRO against the man if you live with him, but not if you don't. (If you want a TRO against a man you don't live with and have not recently lived with, you still need to go to court about something else and get the TRO as part of that action. Talk to a lawyer about how to do that.)

Like a divorce, you can do your own TRO and get it without a lawyer (in some cities). Groups in some areas are working with judges on forms to use in getting a TRO without a lawyer. The court or shelter in your area should know about this.

When you go to court for the TRO you'll need to give the judge the short form or a written, sworn statement describing what the man has done and what you're afraid he'll do.

You'll need to notify the man that you're going to court against him and what you're saying about him. You do this by serving him with a copy of your complaint or statement (affidavit) along with notice of your court date. (Just like in a divorce.) The judge will then hear both your stories and make a decision. In general, courts like to hear both sides of a story before issuing orders about it; but you CAN get a TRO even if your husband or boyfriend doesn't come to court. Tell him that he can't avoid the court's orders by just refusing to show up. Also, if you're in danger and can't wait to notify the man or if you can't find him, you may get a TRO anyway if you can prove to the judge that you are in danger of being hurt now and can't wait. The court will issue a TRO that will only be good a short time—up to two or three weeks—and you must notify the man during that time. He can then ask for the date to be postponed while he gets a lawyer and prepares his case, so you might have to go back to court twice. If you don't notify him before your court date your TRO might be dissolved.

This is a brand new law and the courts in each county have to work out how they're going to handle these TROs. The court in your area may not yet be familiar with the law. Tell them its number is AB 1019 and that it went into effect in January 1978.

How to Enforce a TRO

A restraining order is just a piece of paper signed by a judge. What you do with it determines how effective it'll be in protecting you.

You will get a copy of the order. This is your proof that it exists. If your husband or boyfriend is on probation or parole, send a copy to his PO or parole agent. Notify the man that you have the order, if he doesn't know. If you expect trouble, take or have the court send a copy to your local police station. Explain the situation to them and ask them to come quickly if you call them for help.

TROs are temporary and the police sometimes don't know if the TRO you claim you have is an old one or one still in effect. Some cities, such as San Francisco, have computerized TRO records so that the police can call in and get a report on whether or not a TRO is in force, just like they can call in about traffic ticket warrants. When your TRO expires you can go back to court and get another. If your TRO is part of your divorce it may be good indefinitely, like the support and custody orders. If you need to rely on it for a long time (like six months or more), go back to the court clerk where you got your divorce and have your copy recertified—stamped and dated by the clerk—so the police, POs, etc. will know it's still good.

The police will often refuse to enforce TROs. They will claim that the order is a CIVIL order and must be enforced by the court. If the man violates the order, you CAN go back to court and tell the judge who either can warn the man or send him to jail for contempt of court. However, violating a restraining order is also a CRIMINAL offense (penal code 166.4, a misdemeanor.) You may have the man arrested for violating the order AND go back to court and complain to the judge. (For general ideas on how to deal with the police, see that section of the handbook.) Refusing to enforce a court order is a misdemeanor crime, so get the officers' names and badge numbers and complain if they refuse to help you.

If you have other questions about TROs, call legal aid, the police, or the court that issued yours to you.

Money Problems

If the time comes when you decide that you are going to leave the man you're with, you'll think first about how you're going to be able to make it on your own financially. If you already have a job that pays enough for you and your children to live on, you're lucky. If not, and if your husband is working, when you file for divorce you can ask for temporary support payments for yourself and the children which can get you through the first few months of your separation. (See the section on divorce.)

If you don't have any money, or a job, and you can't get any money from your husband, there are some government programs that will be able to help:

AFDC (welfare)—is available to all women, married or single, with children.

Food Stamps—are available to people below a certain income level, married or single, with or without children.

Medi-Cal—the same is true for Medi-Cal as for Food Stamps.

There are community groups around the Bay Area where people are ready to help you apply for these programs, get training or a job, housing, childcare, or give you food and clothes until you get government aid or a job. In the resource list are some of the places you can call to get help.

Welfare Problems

If you decide to apply for welfare, there are a few things you should watch out for. This is not a complete "how to do it" guide, but some notes on problems you can avoid if you know to watch out for them. Dealing with social service agencies is at least as upsetting and frustrating as dealing with the police or the courts; so you should take a friend or advocate with you to help you fight for the aid you're entitled to.

Paternity

If you are applying for AFDC for the first time in this county, they will ask you for information about the father of your children so they can contact him and collect money for the support of the children. The welfare people will ask you for this information and give it to a section of the District Attorney's office. If you don't know who the father is or say you don't, they will ask you questions about who you were sleeping with at the time the child was conceived. They will also want to know where the father is or the last address you have for him. The DA is not supposed to give your husband or boyfriend any information about you; BUT, she or he will obviously tell him what county you're in. If he's persistent, this information may be enough for him to find you. Women have travelled across the country to escape a man only to have him follow them and search a city top to bottom, forcing them to move again.

If you believe your husband or boyfriend will harass or hurt you if contacted by the DA, you may refuse to give information about him. In some counties there is a special section on the information form for you to check if giving information about the father would not be in the best interests of your children. He does not have to have been convicted of hurting you before, although police reports and medical records documenting this will help your case. If your worker is not sympathetic you can go to the supervisor and then request a fair hearing. You can get help from Welfare Rights or Legal Aid at this stage. The county is not supposed to delay or deny aid while they investigate, if you sign an agreement that you will either cooperate or show good cause why you shouldn't cooperate.

Before you even apply for welfare you should try and talk to a Legal Aid lawyer about if you have good cause. You can also call Welfare Rights and the shelter in your area for support.

Immigration

If you are not a citizen but are here legally as a resident alien, you may be able to apply for welfare, but it may endanger your chances for citizenship later. If you are in the process of applying for resident status or in any way changing your status, you should wait to apply for aid; the government tries to discourage people from coming into the country and getting on public assistance. If you are here illegally, you may endanger yourself by applying for aid. You must show papers when applying for all forms of aid except food stamps. Our information is that food stamp workers are only supposed to ask for proof of citizenship if they have a reason to suspect you are here illegally. Even so, you should check on the practice in your area.

Immigrants here legally and illegally should be very careful and CONSULT IMMIGRATION EXPERTS BEFORE APPLYING FOR ANY TYPE OF AID. YOU MIGHT PUT YOURSELF IN DANGER NOW OR RUIN YOUR CHANCES OF CHANGING YOUR STATUS IN THE FUTURE.

Military Law

More and more of us are starting to feel that there is a relationship between military training and the battering of women—many, many men who are or have been in the military abuse the women they live with. Whether this is caused by violence or sexism of the military needs to be talked about and ways of changing this need to be found.

Very little has been done in the military about domestic violence. There aren't special programs we can tell you to go to; most of us haven't even dealt with the regular legal and social services the military offers. This section is just a basic outline of military law as it affects battered women; we'd like to put out a separate pamphlet in the future on battered women and the military that will contain more complete information.

Who to Call for Help

If you are attacked or are being harassed by a man in the military you can sometimes call the military police and sometimes call the civilian police, depending on whose jurisdiction the attack takes place in. Either the state or the federal government or both will have jurisdiction over where you live (which is probably where that attack takes place). This means that they control that area, and that their police, laws, and courts have power there.

If you live on base you need to find out whose jurisdiction your home is in. There are three possibilities: It could be in state jurisdiction and the city police will enforce the state laws there, or it could be in federal jurisdiction and the military police will enforce military and federal laws there, or it could be under "concurrent" jurisdiction and you can call either police force and they will enforce the law of the group that they work for. The government used to try and have exclusive federal government control over all parts of its military bases. It is moving away from this policy now. The jurisdiction question is settled at the time the base is set up (when the land is bought), which means that old bases still have much of their housing areas under federal jurisdiction.

The Law

The military has its own laws, called the Uniform Code of Military Justice. It's the same for all branches of the service; though each branch and even each base has its own policies, just like each city and each police force has its own policies regarding different crimes. Men who assault women they live with or are married to are charged with assault—there is no wife beating statute in the Military Code.

The Police

If you live off base (and not on government property) you can call the regular city police and follow all the steps outlined in the rest of the handbook. They may want to call the military police or try to not take responsibility for the man, but they CAN arrest him even though he's in the military. (MPs, off base, can also arrest a man and take him into custody if you make a citizen's arrest.)

Convincing military police to arrest a man involves the same steps as convincing civilian police, but is probably harder. There are basically the same guidelines regarding felony and misdemeanor arrests as there are in civilian law. Women can also make citizen's arrests and ask the MPs to take the man away. If anything, MPs probably have more discretion than civilian police in deciding whether or not to arrest a man and who to report him to. Also, military agencies have not been approached and pressured by women's groups so they aren't as sensitive to domestic violence and haven't developed special domestic violence procedures.

Punishment

Whether or not the MPs arrest the man, they can report him. They can report him to the company commander, who can order punishment or send him to a counselor. In the military a man is more likely to actually go to a counselor when ordered to do so than a civilian man is. Or the MPs can give the case to the base legal officer.

The military equivalent of the DA's office is the base legal office (Judge Advocate General in the Army, Navy, and Air Force and Station Legal Officer in the Marines). They use information given them by the military police to make decisions about prosecuting. Their role is not as clear as the DA's however because they advise the Company Commander on legal questions about the case and advise the man of his rights and even represent him at his hearing.

TROs

TROs granted by the state courts may not be enforced by military police because they are not bound by state courts, only by military and federal courts. This varies from base to base, so some bases may cooperate with civilian officials. There is nothing equivalent to TROs in the military system.

Where to Go for Advice

In deciding what legal steps to take in dealing with an abusive military husband or boyfriend, you can get information from the base legal (JAG) officers—they should advise you of your options and how to go about enforcing your rights. Although they are the same people who will also handle your husband's or boyfriend's defense, they are lawyers and are supposed to keep your secrets.

Glossary and Other Things We Get Questions About

California State Victims of Violent Crime Compensation Program: This program pays the expenses of crime victims—medical, childcare, lost wages, etc. It requires that you cooperate with the police and file a police report and that you fill out forms proving what you lost because of the crime. So far this program has not given much money to battered women, not considering them to be true victims. If you do get any money, it will take three to six months and you may get only some of your expenses paid for.

You must be a California resident when the crime occurs. Immigrants here legally are eligible. Women may apply for the losses of their children as well as their own losses. Payments are based on financial need. Some counties have specially trained people to help you fill out the forms (see the resource list). The police and hospital emergency rooms usually have forms or know where to get them.

If you are badly hurt, the man who hurt you was arrested and if you have easily documented bills, this might be a good way to get back some of your money. Just remember that you have to pay it out first.

Civil Suits: A woman can always sue a person she is not related to for loss resulting from injuries to her body or property. Children can also sue strangers. Civil suits are more complicated when the people involved are related, however, even if no longer living together as a family. Some states still do not allow a wife to sue her husband except in special circumstances. About half the states, including California, DO allow suits between family members.

In California, a woman can sue her husband for injuries to her body or property or injuries to her children. We mention this because we get questions about it; we don't recommend it. For one thing, you are still working within the legal system and have the same problems of proof and witnesses as in criminal cases. Civil cases take much longer than criminal cases—it could literally take a few years to complete your case. Attorney fees would take a large portion of your settlement; and you can only collect what the man has—in other words, it only makes sense to sue men who are fairly well off.

If you have injuries or losses that you can easily prove and if these injuries were caused by a man who can actually pay a settlement, you might go talk to an attorney about bringing a suit. Although we think a civil suit would be a large drain on your time and energy, if you still want to try it you may help develop a new area in civil law.

Immigration: At some time in the future we'd like to put out a separate handbook on the legal problems and rights of immigrant women. In the meantime we urge immigrant women to consult with immigration experts before taking any legal action.

We want to make a further statement about dealing with immigrant men who are here illegally. We have included no section in this handbook on how to turn a man in to the immigration authorities. This is because we don't believe in using the immigration system to deal with battering men, and we've chosen not to cooperate with women who want to have men deported. We don't feel good about using a system that mainly harasses people.

Glossary

Missing Persons: Women are sometimes afraid their husbands or boyfriends will report them missing to the police if they leave home. Every adult woman, married or single, has the right to move around freely. The police will not hunt you down and drag you home. If they run across you and recognize you as someone reported missing, you can explain the situation to them and go on your way. If they try and talk you into going home, you don't have to listen to them. If you are nervous, you can call the missing persons bureau of your police department yourself and tell them that you are not missing. You don't have to tell the police where you are going or staying if you are afraid that they will tell your husband or boyfriend. In a large city, police usually have other things to do besides look for missing persons unless it looks like someone has been hurt or kidnapped.

If you take your children with you, read the section on child custody.

Peace Bonds: In domestic violence situations, a woman would get a lawyer, go to court and try and get a judge to make the man who's bothering her put up money for a peace bond. (It doesn't matter if the woman is married to the man or not.) The judge would list what the man had to do in order not to lose the money. For instance, the judge could order the man to stay away from the woman's house or order that the man not hit the woman. If the man did any of these things, the woman could go back to court, and if she could convince the judge of what happened, the man would lose the money.

We get a lot of questions about peace bonds, but we don't recommend them or know where people hear about them. (We're not even sure you can get them in California.) They are very expensive—the woman asking for the bond must hire a lawyer (Legal Aid probably won't do this for you) and post money for a bond herself. There is no guarantee that the judge will agree to ask the man for the bond or that the man will care if he loses the money. Finally, after all your time and money, you really don't get any new protections from peace bonds.

Subpoena: A subpoena is an order from the court telling you to come in and tell what you know. It may be mailed or handed to you.

It should say in the corner what kind of hearing you are being asked to come to—a preliminary hearing or a trial. (See section on pressing charges.) Call the District Attorney's office the day before the hearing to make sure you still have to go. Make sure and call if you can't go because of sickness, an accident, etc. If you don't show up, charges against the man could be dropped and you could be in trouble with the court. If you get a subpoena and don't want to or are afraid to go to court, call and talk to the DA and read the section on pressing charges.

APPENDIX B

SUGGESTIONS FOR PUBLIC POLICIES

Prepared by

Donna M. Moore

Although the plight of battered women is difficult, at best, a number of recent meetings and publications have addressed themselves to solutions for the problems of battered women (Battered Women: Issues of Public Policy, 1978; A Study of Spouse Battering in Montana, 1978). Following is a series of suggestions regarding solutions for battered women. These suggestions were developed at the Battered Women's Conference sponsored at the University of California, Davis by the Women's Resources and Research Center in February 1978. It is important that the reader remember, however, that these are suggestions and must be modified to work best within specific geographic areas depending on already existing laws, services, funding, and human resources.

Criminal Justice System

Since *law enforcement officers* are called upon to intervene in domestic disturbance calls and often respond ineffectively, police departments should provide mandatory training to officers regarding appropriate responses to such calls. Trainers must include women who can educate law enforcement officers regarding the myths and realities of battering as well as provide information regarding local feminist referral resources available to both the police department and battered women. The police departments should establish domestic violence intervention teams in cooperation with local women's groups. Police departments must be accountable to the victims as well as the perpetrators and must therefore remove one of the parties from the home for an extended period of time which will ensure physical safety for the victim. Law enforcement officers must be mandated to (1) inform the victim of her rights; (2) inform the victim of community, medical, and legal resources available to her; (3) inform her of the process for making a citizen's arrest; (4) inform her of the criminal justice process in a neutral manner rather than in a manner which actively discourages her taking legal steps against her partner; (5) actively enforce temporary restraining orders; and (6) report each domestic violence incident in order that accurate public records can be maintained regarding the number of such events.

District attorneys and judges should be required to attend training sessions on domestic violence which would include women trainers who can educate such persons regarding the myths and realities of battering and inform them regarding local feminist referral resources. District attorneys offices should be encouraged to provide an advocate to work with victims throughout the prosecution in cases of battering so that the victim will not drop the charges. District attorneys must also work actively to gain the expertise and experience in winning such cases in court. Judges must be encouraged to take domestic violence seriously and appropriately sentence convicted batterers.

Law schools should provide mandatory courses regarding domestic violence in order that future lawyers and judges will have more accurate information regarding such issues.

Each state *legislature* should be asked to appoint a committee both to review all existing laws which would affect, or neglect, battered women and to hold public hearings in the area of domestic violence which would propose alternatives to the existing law. Legislation should be enacted to eliminate the filing fee for obtaining a temporary restraining order and to require that all public agencies keep accurate records regarding spouse abuse, similar to the records required for cases of abused children.

Feminists should research legislators' voting histories and attitudes and work actively for the election and appointment of persons who are supportive of sensitive treatment of battered women.

Social Service Agencies

Since each county and community already has in existence public and private social service agencies which offer some of the services needed by a battered woman, a paid advocate is needed to represent the battered woman's needs to all local agencies, to work to develop sensitivity to these needs in individuals in all social service agencies, and to identify needs of battered women which cannot be met by existing agencies, as well as to educate the community regarding the necessity of creating new resources for unmet needs. A specific plan should be developed, under the coordination of this advocate, to bring together representatives of all agencies to discuss and identify services which are available and how these services can be pooled to meet the multiple needs of battered women and batterers.

Agencies should prepare and distribute a pamphlet describing both the long-term and short-term services available for the battered woman. These pamphlets should be made available to all social service agencies for referral purposes and to the public at large. Social services should offer their expertise in proposal writing and identifying potential funding sources for those attempting to set up shelters. A general crisis line, responsive to battered women, should be created in all counties with workers trained to assist battered women. Such a line should be widely publicized through the media by public service messages. Social service agency workers should be educated regarding various aspects of family counseling, including how to prevent battering in ongoing relationships and how to counsel the woman who chooses to leave her home. Battered women must be eligible for criminal justice funds available to victims of other violent crimes and there should be funds for specialized personnel in public agencies to respond to the needs of battered women. Welfare money must be made available on an emergency basis within one working day of application by battered women.

Emergency Room Staffs and Physicians

Since *emergency rooms* are frequently the first contact for battered women, it is important to develop a mandatory protocol for suspected wife battering similar to that provided for child abuse and rape. These protocols must gather data which will be reported annually to state and federal officials in order that accurate information can be gathered regarding the incidence of battering. The suspected victim should be offered a supportive advocate to be present for the duration of her stay in the emergency room. The emergency room staff (including doctors, nurses, social workers, and others) should be educated and sensitized to the problems of domestic violence through training provided by or approved by local battered women's groups. The schools in the medical professions should be required to teach mandatory classes regarding the psychological and physical dynamics of battering and how to best treat such victims. Victims should have the right to request a female physician, whenever available, in the emergency room. Victims should be referred to community support systems while still in the emergency room, a wallet-size card with community support system information (telephone numbers, contact persons, and services) should be provided to each suspected victim of battering. Information should also be available to the batterer regarding community support services appropriate to his needs.

Since *private physicians* are frequently the first contact for middle-class battered women, a mandatory protocol for suspected wife battering should be developed specific to private practice, similar to that available for child abuse and rape victims reporting to emergency rooms.

Personal Support for the Victim

It must be recognized that a woman who has been involved in a battering relationship needs a personal support system in order to discuss alternatives to her present situation, to leave the battering relationship, to enter a shelter, or to establish herself independently. She also often needs to receive continuing support long after she has left the battering relationship. In order to begin meeting these needs, county task forces should be established which are composed of representatives from public agencies and grass root organizations to explore the needs and make recommendations to appropriate funds to meet the needs of battered women. Funding for programs for battered women should be seen as a legitimate ongoing social service need and should be made available on an ongoing basis through both government and private funding agencies. Money should be made available for large-scale educational projects to teach both the community at large and personnel working for shelters regarding the personal support needs of battered women in order that the entire community can most appropriately respond to those needs.

Setting up a Shelter

Since shelters for battered women have been a cornerstone of women working against violence against women, both recognition of and funding for shelters must be forthcoming on the community, state, and federal level. A national clearinghouse should be devised to establish and share reserves and resource organizations; an updated publication of current shelter status and program development should be produced annually. Legislation should be enacted to create "battered spouses" as a distinct class for both reporting and funding purposes. Shelters should be allowed maximum self-determination and a minimum of interference from other agencies, including funding agencies. Community organization for support services for battered women should consist of two coalitions: a core group of women helping women and a secondary coalition composed of community service organizations (criminal justice, social service, mental health, and others). Eventually, shelters should be predominantly run by the battered women themselves. The problem of battered women is not of an experimental nature, but rather an already documented problem that demands recognition, action, and funding and must be treated as such by both private and public agencies. The definition of the displaced homemaker should be expanded to include battered women of any age, with or without children.

Churches

Since religious leaders are often the persons to whom battered women turn for counseling, training should be provided for these persons in order that they can most appropriately work with such women. Further, churches must recognize the role they often have in creating an atmosphere conducive to battering by both implicitly and explicitly teaching that a man has the right to control his wife and children; once this is recognized, churches should use local advocates for battered women as recourses for new ways of teaching family relationships without encouraging battering.

Education

Since traditional sex-role socialization plays a major role in the development of battering relationships (Martin, 1976; Roy, 1977) and since the educational system plays a major role in socializing American children, schools must begin seriously examining their curriculum, curriculum materials, and textbooks to ensure that they are not socializing sexist attitudes which encourage behaviors and attitudes supportive of battering relationships. Schools must eliminate use of corporal punishment which acts as a model for solving disagreements via physical abuse. Communities must work actively for the inclusion of family life and sexuality courses in all school systems which teach alternate sex-role models and must work for vigorous enforcement and implementation of nonsexist classes and teachers. These classes must act as preventative measures through presentation of information about violence in the home and resources available to battered women and children.

Since women exiting a battering situation often find themselves lacking in skills to support themselves or their families, continuing education programs should be expanded which include career and personal counseling, academic and job training, and job hunting skills. Further, since the difficulties women experience both during and after leaving a battering situation often relate to her ability to communicate her feelings and needs to others, both educational institutions and community service programs should provide free assertiveness training and other communication programs for all students and clients.

Media

Since men and women have often been presented in the media as unsatisfactory role models and many of these roles promote an acceptance of violence and sexism in our society, television networks should develop programs which depict people in both nonviolent and nonsexist lifestyles; products of manufacturers who sponsor violent and sexist television programs should be boycotted; pressure should be applied to the Federal Communications Commission to remove sexist and violent programs and commercials; equal and prime time should be allotted to feminists by all forms of media to present their views; and the media should be encouraged to cover conferences, shelters, and other issues regarding battered women.

Mental Health

Since mental health practitioners and agencies should be accountable to clientele who are mostly women and often the victims of violence perpetrated by men, all schools training mental health professionals should institute mandatory courses regarding domestic violence; these courses should be taught by or developed in consultation with battered women's advocates and should be prerequisite to professional licensing. Existing mental health agencies and practitioners must be sensitized to these issues and be prepared to effectively work against violence against women. The mental health profession should mandate that a feminist therapist serve on the staff of all agencies funded by public monies and feminist therapists must be given positive recognition by both the mental health profession and the public. Battered women must not receive prolonged and excessive administration of psychotropic drugs in lieu of other assistance.

Since the negative effects of both sex-role stereotyping by therapists and sexual contact between clients and therapists have been well documented (Chesler, 1972; Butler and Zelen, 1977), the mental health profession and the criminal justice system must take strong action against any therapist having sexual relations with a client.

Marriage and Family

Since the traditional family structure and its rigid sex roles often prevent realization of individual full potentials and options, funds should be provided for research and exploration of creative and alternative lifestyles less conducive to abusive relationships. Funds should be provided for 24-hour day care centers. Housework should be recognized through compensation, including both wages and social security. National legislation should be enacted to protect women from sexual and physical assaults in all cohabiting situations. Premarital counseling should be required and should include development of clear marital expectations between both partners, information regarding rights and loss of rights which will occur as a result of marriage, information regarding alternatives to traditional marital relationships, and the writing of a marriage contract between the two parties.

Children of Battered Women

Since there is general consensus but little substantial documentation regarding the negative effects of domestic violence on children, including its cyclical effects, special programs should be funded and implemented to include research, crisis intervention, long-term support, and development of practical solutions. Shelters for battered women must include space for children of the residents as well as parenting classes for mothers who might need to develop or redevelop nurturing relationships with their children. Counseling services must be provided by both shelters and public agencies for children of battered women. The criminal justice system must recognize and attend to the needs of children in making decisions regarding family separation, child custody, or child visitation. Studies must be made regarding the effects of visitation by the noncustodial parent, including the use of neutral pick-up places and supervised and evaluated visitations. Whenever a child's history is taken by schools, social service agencies, or medical facilities, it should include inquiry into battering within the family.

In summary, every segment of society must take responsibility for recognizing that battering occurs and exploring how it might be able to decrease battering and respond to the needs of an entire family unit: the battered woman, her batterer, and her children.

References

Battered Women: Issues of Public Policy (1978) A consultation sponsored by the U.S. Commission on Civil Rights, Washington, D.C., January 30-31.

BUTLER, S. and S. ZELEN (1977) "Sexual intimacies between therapists and patients." Psychotherapy: Theory, Research & Practice 14(2).

CHESLER, P. (1972) Women and Madness. New York: Doubleday.

MARTIN, D. (1976) Battered Wives. San Francisco: Glide Publications.

ROY, M. (1977) Battered Women. New York: Litton.

Study of Spouse Battering in Montana (1978) Helena, MT: Department of Community Affairs.

APPENDIX C

BIBLIOGRAPHY OF MATERIALS ON BATTERED WOMEN

Prepared by

Jane Iddings
Karen Mack
Donna M. Moore

Following are some sources of information and readings regarding battered women. This list is far from inclusive but attempts to cite sources for basic information, major books, "how to" publications, and bibliographies for those who wish to pursue the topic further.

BOOKS—GENERAL INFORMATION

Anderson, George. "Wives, Mothers, and Victims" *America,* **August 6, 1977 pp. 46-50.**

Anderson discusses reasons why wives stay on with husbands who beat them: fear and economic status. Children are also an important factor for not leaving. He mentions that in England the public awareness seems to be more empathetic toward battered women than in the United States. Issue not confined to the lower economic strata of our society. Alcohol is a frequent factor. Childhood experiences in battering husbands all similar: child abuse in own families or parental violence. Discusses achievements of the feminist movement with battered women. Anderson also describes proposed legislation concerning battered wives.

Bard, Morton. The function of the police in crisis intervention and conflict management: A training manual. Washington, D.C.: Dept. of Justice, Law Enforcement Assistance Administration, 1975.

It discusses the ideas behind crisis intervention and methods for its implementation by police departments, how to organize field training programs and developing forms and procedures. Describes actual cases.

"Battered Wives: Help for the Victim Next Door," *MS.,* **5 #2 (August 1976), pp. 95-98.**

A collection of several short articles dealing with different aspects of wife abuse. Contained is a general overview, a case history, a legal overview, a review of *Scream Quietly of the Neighbors Will Hear* by Erin Pizzey and discussion of Great Britain's experience. The article also contains a description of Rainbow Retreat, a refuge in Phoenix, Arizona, a state-by-state listing of sources, a short bibliography, and a list of upcoming conventions dealing with the topic.

Bell, Joseph. "Rescuing the Battered Wife," *Human Behavior,* **June 1977, pp. 16-23.**

This consists mostly of Bell's accounts with professionals in the field of social services: Gordon Markie at Pasadena Mental Health Center and Barbara Star at University of California at Santa Barbara. Bell also discusses a study done by Elizabeth Truninger on the legal aspects of marital violence. She postulates reasons why women put up with the battering. Bell writes about his contacts with women at a shelter. He talks about the awareness the movement is bringing to the public, such as a new breed of socially orientated police trained in domestic violence and victims of abuse are looking for new alternatives.

Colorado Advisory Committee to the U.S. Commission on Civil Rights. *The Silent Victims: Denver's Battered Women.* **22 pgs. 1977, free. Order from: Publications Management Division, U.S. Commission on Civil Rights, 1121 Vermont Ave. NW, Washington, D.C. 10425.**

The purpose of this study was to generate primary data on the battering of women and the options open to them as they seek police protection, legal assistance, refuge housing, and other social services. The report reviews the literature, discusses the victim, the incidence of assault on women, and law enforcement response, as well as the prosecutorial response. Contains recommendations for further action. A 13 minute color film entitled "A Woman, A Spaniel and A Walnut Tree" accompanies the report. Can be viewed free by contacting the above address.

"Black and Blue Marriages," *Human Behavior,* **June 1976, pp. 47-48.**

A review of the study done by J. J. Gayford, a consulting psychiatrist in Surrey, England. Gayford did research with 100 women who had been beaten by their husbands. He compiled his data into patterns of violence with alcoholism and crime. He concluded that for the women he interviewed, their social life revolved around men who were drinkers and gamblers, thus leading to the tendency for abusive relationships. Gayford also states that something needs to be done in the way of shelter and care for the children involved in these families or they will become future batterers/beaten wives.

Gelles, Richard J. "Abused Wives: Why Do They Stay?" *Journal of Marriage and the Family,* **38 #10 (November 1976).**

Results of a study conducted on 80 families. Paper discusses the research method and sample (which is a *non*representative sample) and suggests the following: increase in severity and frequency of abuse influences decisions to obtain divorce or outside intervention; those who were abused as children will more likely tolerate abuse as adults; lack of economic independence and powerlessness affects decision to leave or seek help. Additionally, outside help is ineffective in coping with intrafamily violence and social constraints and training hamper efforts to change the situation. Bibliography.

"The Paralysis of the Battered Wife," *Human Behavior,* **May 1977, pp. 47-48.**

A study was done by Richard J. Gelles with 41 New Hampshire families in which the wife had been beaten. This article describes the research. Key factors that seemed to influence a woman's decision to fight back were isolated. Yet, there was no simple explanation for the woman's reluctance to leave her situation, other than fear.

Langley, Roger and Richard Levy. *Wife Beating: The Silent Crisis.* **New York: Dutton, April 1977.**

The authors provide an introduction to the social problem of domestic violence. They have interviewed doctors, lawyers, and judges, and they present materials from sociologists, criminologists, and psychologists. Their chapters define the problem, the offender, and the victim, and present vivid case histories that give added dimensions to the problem. The last chapter presents alternatives for women who have to deal with social agencies and the courts as they seek solutions to domestic violence.

Lisa Leghorn. "Social Responses to Battered Women," Part Two. *FAAR Newsletter,* **May/June 1977, pp. 15-19.**

People's analyses of why the problem occurs, affects *how* they respond. We need to identify our social system as part of the problem—we need to see our actions in a political perspective, for example, adequate legislation for protection. The solution of refuges is only a Band Aid station; they need to be accompanied by *widespread* social change, *to prevent beatings in the first place.* Our male-dominated culture has defined the roles for women in the home and the conditions outside the home. The question is not always *what* exactly are we working on, but *how* we are doing it. Must share information with each other on how we have dealt with this problem, in order to educate people; it must be combined with political action, however. Women need *power* to effect the changes that are needed.

Martin, Del. *Battered Wives.* **San Francisco: Glide Publications, 1976 and New York: Pocket Books, 1977.**

First major book published in the United States on wife beating written from a feminist perspective. Focuses on wife-beating in the larger context of male aggression against women, sex-role stereotypes, and the impact of the women's movement. Using the testimony of the victims themselves, the author discusses the marriage structure, the characteristics of the wife beater, the reasons that the wife stays, and the failure of the legal system and of social services. Suggests possible remedies for the victims.

"Men and Violence"; a transcript of a taped consciousness raising session, Fall 1970. Produced for WBHI FM Radio in New York City. *Notes From the Third Year: Women's Liberation.* Pages 39-43.

Seven women discuss their own experiences with men and abuse; how they reacted emotionally in the situation, why they accepted the mistreatings, etc. "We have internalized our fear of invoking male anger, and that we carry around within us this powerlessness."

Michigan Women's Commission. *Domestic Assault: A Report on Family Violence in Michigan.* **141 pgs. 1977, free. Order from: Michigan Women's Commission, 815 Washington Square Bldg., Lansing, MI 48933.**

The Women's Commission held hearings throughout the state of Michigan to obtain testimony that would reflect the scope of the problem. The report is a journal of experiences not only of the victims but of those who have tried to help them. It is also a catalog of suggestions, theories, and recommendations with appendices that include resource organizations and agencies and an up-to-date bibliography.

Parnas, Raymond. "Police Discretion and Diversion of Incidents of Intra-Family Violence," Law and Contemporary Problems, Vol. 36, No. 4 (Autumn 1971), p. 538.

This is an outline of some current police practices.

Pizzey, Erin. *Scream Quietly or the Neighbors Will Hear.* **Ridley Enslow Publishers, Box 301, Short Hills, NJ 07078. $7.95**

Pizzey's book is the story behind the founding of Chiswick Women's Aid, one of the first shelters for battered women. Much of the book is case histories of the first women who passed through the shelter but it also tells of the battles that had to be fought with indifferent public agencies. Pizzey concludes with a plan for future action.

Pogrebin, Letty Cotlin. "Do Women Make Men Violent?" *MS.,* **3 #5 (November 1974), pp. 49-52+.**

This article deals with one of the more prevalent beliefs held justifying wife abuse. It asserts that male aggression is encouraged during childhood and that this male self-image requires reaffirmation. Additionally, the article deals with statistics and incidences of women in violent situations and the theory of victimology. It reviews several books and articles on men/women relations and violence and maintains a strong feminist viewpoint throughout. The author states that women do not precipitate violence and that strong feminist leaders are needed to change social posture on this issue.

Response. **Washington, D.C. Center for Women Policy Studies.**

Bimonthly newsletter to keep groups working on domestic violence and sexual assault informed of current literature, funding sources, current research, conferences, and, most importantly, on innovative and effective programs and techniques.

Rockwood, Marcia. "Courts and Cops—Enemies of Battered Wives?" *MS.,* **April 1977, p. 19.**

Discusses the action suit filed last December in Manhattan Supreme Court by a coalition of New York-based legal organizations. The charges are as follows: "police deny the existence, prevalence, and seriousness of violence against married women or treat it as a private privilege of marital discipline." A similar suit was filed in California by Legal Aid Society in Alameda County.

Roy, Maria, ed. *Battered Wives.* **New York: Van Nostrand-Reinhold, 1977.**

The collection includes articles by psychologists, sociologists, law enforcement officials, and authorities from community programs. The book begins with a concise history of wife beating and illustrates how our culture has tolerated and condoned the use of physical force to resolve marital conflicts. It then presents a survey of 150 wife beating cases, examines the social dynamics of the battering syndrome, and explains the cyclical pattern of children repeating their parents' behavior. The book addresses the questions most frequently asked about wife beating, "Why do women stay with men who abuse them?" and "What is the role of drugs, alcohol, sexual, and financial stress?" Descriptions of the men and women involved in violent relationships are explored by psychologists, and one neurological theory of violence is presented. The legal aspects of wife battering are covered, but they pertain mostly to New York state, which has a system of family courts that differs from most other jurisdictions. The most valuable portion of the book is the last section on future trends and legislative needs. Roy proposes a model for services, and a sociological perspective of prevention and treatment of wife beating is offered by Dr. Murray Straus.

Schonborn, Karl. To Keep the Peace: Crisis Management in Law Enforcement. 1976: National Conference of Christians and Jews, 809 Central Tower Building, San Francisco, CA 94103. Pages 19-23.

Charts all police departments with family crisis units and compares them across a number of dimensions.

Search, Gay. "London: Battered Wives," *MS. Magazine,* June 1974, pp. 24-26.

An interview with Erin Pizzey, founder of the Women's Aid in Chiswick, London, a shelter for battered wives. The article consists of a description of the shelter, exerpts from some of the women living in the refuge, and comments about the lack of legal cooperation in England. The conclusion stated: "what's really needed is legal and societal recognition of the problem."

Steinmetz, Suzanne K., ed. *The Cycle of Violence: Assertive, Aggressive, and Abusive Family Interaction.* New York: Praeger Publishers, 1977.

Steinmetz, using conflict theory, resource theory, and social learning theory, traces the patterns of conflict resolution found in 57 intact urban and suburban families. Her research shows that each family assumes a consistent pattern for resolving conflict, often related to stages in the family life cycle; and that all patterns of conflict resolution, whether assertive, aggressive, or abusive, are passed on from one generation to the next. A family using physical force to settle conflict instills in its offspring the belief that physical force is a socially acceptable method for resolving conflict, thus perpetuating a "cycle of violence." Steinmetz has also included an examination of the relationship of intrafamily violence to a wide range of other criminally violent acts and a controversial finding on the extent of husband battering. The book, well documented and referenced, is a scholarly research handbook for the student of domestic violence.

Steinmetz, Suzanne and Murray Straus, eds. *Violence in the Family*. New York: Harper and Row, 1974.

This collection of research on family violence has six scholarly articles on the origins and patterns of spousal violence including studies of violence in divorce-prone families, spouses as murder victims, and the role of laws and courts in limiting wife abuse.

Straus, Murray A., Richard J. Gelles, and Suzanne K. Steinmetz, "Violence in the Family: An Assessment of Knowledge and Needs," presented to the American Association for the Advancement of Science, Boston, February 23, 1976, 51 pages.

The paper concludes that extensive study is indicated in both theoretical and empirical realms. Violence appears to be far more extensive than expected in areas of child and spouse abuse, but statistics are scanty and unreliable. Some theories of interpersonal violence are discussed as well as the progress of so-called victimology research. There is a short segment on abuse in relation to the criminal justice system and problems the authors consider to be in immediate need of attention. Extensive bibliography.

Truninger, Elizabeth. Marital violence: the legal solutions. *Hastings Law Journal,* November 23, 1971, pp. 259-276.

Examination of California laws and procedures available for dealing with marital violence (short of murder) from criminal statutes such as assault and battery to civil procedures and their potential and application. Although it discusses California laws, the fact that other states' laws follow similar principles makes this article broadly applicable. The explanation of legal terms is extremely helpful.

U.S. Work Projects Administration. Iowa. "The Legal Status of Women From 2250 B.C." Des Moines, Iowa: Attorney General's Office, 1938.

This is an exhaustive translation of laws pertaining to all aspects of womens' lives. Mesopotamian, Chinese, Biblical, Hindu, Greek, Roman, and Medieval major texts and codes are all included. All aspects are covered including under what level of punishment allowed. Also included were punishments to be dealt to men who overstep these bounds and under what circumstances women could claim unjust treatment. An *unexcelled* comparative historical survey.

Warrior, Betsy. *Working on Wife Abuse.* 46 Pleasant St., Cambridge, MA 02139. $3.00 + 50¢ postage. 40% off on 10 or more, fourth edition, 111 pages.

An outstanding directory of coalitions, task forces, groups, and individuals working to offer support, refuges, and services to battered women. Lists publications pertinent to the issue including: books, films, research studies, need and statistical reports, theses, posters, pamphlets, speeches, funding sources, etc. Also contains an introduction examining the history and purposes of refuges.

Western States Shelter Network Newsletter. SFNLAF, 1095 Market St., Room 417, San Francisco, CA 94103.

Information regarding shelters, needs, legislation, etc., in the Western states.

BIBLIOGRAPHIES

"The Battered Woman, A Bibliography," Alcohol, Drug Abuse, and Mental Health Administrtion, Office of Communications and Public Affairs, 5600 Fishers Lane, Rockville, MD 20850.

Center for Women Policy Studies, 2000 P St. NW, Suite 508, Washington, D.C. 20036. "Spouse Abuse: An Annotated Bibliography."

They have established a clearinghouse of information and a listing of resources persons, publish an *outstanding bibliography and a very fine newsletter.*

"A Comprehensive Bibliography: Part One: Domestic Violence, Center for Women Policy Studies, 2000 P St. NW, Suite 508, Washington, D.C. 20036; Part Two: Crisis Intervention, Domestic Violence Research Project, Police Department, Kansas City, Missouri." Center for Women Policy Studies, 2000 P St. NW, Suite 508, Washington, D.C. 20036.

Lystad, Mary, ed. *Violence at Home: An annotated bibliography.* Rockville, MD: National Institute of Mental Health, 1974. DHEW Publication No. (ADM) 75-136. Stock number 1724-00398.

Abstracts of research studies on violence among family members, largely those published in the last 10 years. Conclusions of the studies are given in the abstracts making them particularly useful. Of Primary interest is the section on violence among husbands and wives, pp. 27-31.

McShane, Claudette. *Annotated bibliography on woman battering.* July 1977. Available from: The Midwest Parent Child Welfare Resource Center, School of Social Welfare, University of Wisconsin, P.O. Box 413, Milwaukee, Wisconsin 53201. Single copies free, multiple copies 25¢ each.

Includes references to academic research, clinical reports on therapeutic interventions, feminist writings, and recommendations for amelioration of domestic violence. Reference to listings of women working on wife abuse as well as handbooks available to assist those wishing to begin projects.

Straus, Murray. "A Bibliography: Family Violence Research Program," University of New Hampshire, Department of Sociology, Durham 03824, September, 1975 (25¢ per copy).

U.S. Department of Health, Education and Welfare, National Institute of Mental Health, National Clearinghouse, "Bibliography: 'Battered Spouses'," Rockville, MD: DHEW, NIMH, National Clearinghouse, computer printout, November 1976.

This is a computer listing which the National Clearinghouse makes available upon request of all items under the subject heading of battered spouses contained in the National Clearinghouse's data archives as of November 1976. Seventeen items are included and annotated, giving author, title, procurement address, source, and bibliographic date, with annotation of the content.

"HOW TO" SOURCES

Duncan, Darlene. *Handbook for battered, abused women.* 34 pgs., 1977. $3.50. Order from CAN-DU Publications, 6331 Hollywood Blvd., Suite 200, Hollywood, CA 90028.

This booklet is designed for the woman who is afraid to seek help or is in a community where no help exists for abused women. The booklet covers alternatives a woman can choose among in deciding on a course of action and includes exercises in evaluating one's feelings.

Fields, Marjory D. and Lehman, Elyse. *A handbook for beaten women:* How to get help if your husband or boyfriend beats you. Brooklyn Legal Services Corp., Brooklyn, NY 11201.

This handbook is aimed at New York residents but is an outstanding model. It includes medical, legal, emotional, financial, and other pertinent information.

Fotjik, Kathleen. *How to develop a wife assault task force and project.* Ann Arbor, MI: NOW Domestic Violence Project, 1976. $1.50.

Step-by-step guide to establishing a structure for aiding victims of wife abuse. Detailed information on organizing, housing, surveying social service agencies, documenting incidence, and sample questionnaires are given in the appendices.

Friedman, Kathleen. *Battered Women: Manual for Survival.* Baltimore, MD: Women's Law Center, 2225 North Charles St., Baltimore, MD 21218. 50¢, 1976.

A 14-page booklet listing resources in Baltimore and describing available legal and counseling options for victims. Advice on how to proceed in situations when police officers and counselors are not helpful.

Gentzler, Rie, ed. *Advocacy Programs for Abused Women.* **1977. To order, write: Rie Gentzler, 2920 Spring Valley Road, Lancaster, PA 17601. Payment $5.00 must accompany the order.**

Rie, working with the Pennsylvania Coalition Against Domestic Violence, has written a practical guide on how to set up a community program for battered women and their children. The manual begins with the basics, assuring the reader that there is no single first step, but three or four aspects of programming that must be considered before a group makes a service commitment. Helpful suggestions include methods for a needs assessment, model shelter budgets, sources of funding to explore, and the steps necessary for incorporation, community support, and an organizational framework. The manual goes on to outline services that may be offered, such as hotlines, shelter, counseling and accompaniment, and special considerations for children and volunteer staffing. An evaluation section is included as well as sample forms.

Resnick, Mindy. *Counselor Training Manual #1.* **Ann Arbor, MI: NOW Domestic Violence Project, 1976. $2.00.**

Guide for counselors advising victims of wife abuse. Discusses the roles of the counselor as practical helper and educator, advocate and supporter, counseling techniques, and the conflicting emotions the victim feels.

APPENDIX D

QUESTIONNAIRE:
EXPERIENCES WITH AND OPINIONS
ABOUT BATTERING

Prepared for the
Battered Women's Conference
sponsored by the Women's Resources
and Research Center at the
University of California, Davis
in February 1978.

The following questions are intended to help us evaluate this conference, plan future programs, and plan both services and research around the issues related to battered women. Please answer the questions thoughtfully and completely so they can be useful to us. Thank you.

1. What is your sex: Female _____ Male _____ 2. What is your age? _____

3. What is your occupation _____

4. What is your education level: less than high school _____ ;

   high school _____ ; some college _____ ; BA/BS _____ ; MA/MS _____ ;

   Ph.D. _____ ; other _____

5. What was the major factor in your attending this conference? Please check one:

   _____ Current job related (I thought it would help me in my work)

   _____ Future job related (I wish to work with battered women in the future)

   _____ Academic (I wanted information for current/future classes)

   _____ Informational (I feel it is a topic everyone needs to know more about)

   _____ Personal (I or a friend has been battered and I felt it might help me)

   _____ Curiousity

   _____ Other _____

6. What expectations did you bring with you to the conference?

   _____

   _____

7. Were those expectations met? If not, please tell us why?

   _____

   _____

Please answer the following questions by circling one response which best indicates your own feeling or experience:

The major cause of battering is:

Socialization   Male Superiority   The man's attitudes
   patterns   in this society   toward women

The woman's attitudes
   or behaviors

Other (Please explain) _____

The major reason battering continues is:

Socialization   Responses of   Responses   The man's
   patterns   public agencies   of courts   attitudes

The woman's attitudes
   or behavior

Other (Please explain) _____

While it is important to provide help for the battered woman, nothing needs to be done to assist the male batterer:

Strongly agree   Agree   Undecided   Disagree   Strongly Disagree

I have been the victim of battering as an adult:

Frequently   Occasionally   Once   Never

I was the victim of battering as a child:

Frequently   Occasionally   Once   Never

I have battered my partner/spouse:

Frequently   Occasionally   Once   Never

I have battered my child(ren):

Frequently   Occasionally   Once   Never

I have feared being physically hurt by a member of the opposite sex:

Frequently   Occasionally   Once   Never

Child visitation rights should be denied the battering spouse:

Strongly agree   Agree   Undecided   Disagree   Strongly Disagree

I have battered an animal or pet:

Frequently   Occasionally   Once   Never

When an inadequate response of law enforcement officers occurs, it is due to:

Fear of injury   Lack of training   The attitude that it
                                              is a private affair

The attitude regarding
  a male's prerogative

It is important to provide information regarding alternatives to battered women:

Strongly agree   Agree   Undecided   Disagree   Strongly Disagree

It is more important to work with abused children than with battered women:

Strongly agree   Agree   Undecided   Disagree   Strongly Disagree

While we should give women information regarding their alternatives, family violence should remain a private affair to be resolved by the parties involved:

Strongly agree   Agree   Undecided   Disagree   Strongly Disagree

I have been afraid that I would physically harm a member of the opposite sex:

Frequently   Occasionally   Once   Never

As a child did you ever observe your parents, or other family members in violent physical altercations?

Frequently   Occasionally   Once   Never

If we could solve the problems of alcohol abuse, the problems of domestic violence would be nearly solved:

Strongly agree   Agree   Undecided   Disagree   Strongly Disagree

Police departments, medical facilities and public social service agencies should have a protocol for handling cases of battered spouses which are similar to those already existing for child abuse:

Strongly agree   Agree   Undecided   Disagree   Strongly Disagree

It should be required that public agencies report suspected spouse abuse, just as they are required to report child abuse:

Strongly agree   Agree   Undecided   Disagree   Strongly Disagree

Medical, legal, law enforcement, and other public social service agency personnel should be required to attend a course regarding spousal abuse in order to better equip themselves with information regarding the problems as well as information regarding solutions:

Strongly agree   Agree   Undecided   Disagree   Strongly Disagree

NOTES

Notes to Introduction

1. See Michigan's Women's Commission, *Domestic Assault: A Report on Family Violence in Michigan* (Lansing: State of Michigan, 1977).

2. See Roger Langley and Richard C. Levy, *Wife Beating: The Silent Crisis* (New York: E. P. Dutton, 1977) and Maria Roy (ed.), *Battered Women: A Psychosociological Study of Domestic Violence* (New York: Van Nostrand, 1977).

3. Marjorie Fields, Notes from the Women's Rights Project, Abused Women, *ACLU*, Vol. 1, No. 8, Nov. 1977, 14 pp.

4. Fields, ibid.

5. Michigan's Women's Commission, ibid.

6. Darlene Duncan, *Handbook for Battered, Abused Women* (Hollywood, Ca.: Can-du Publications, 1977).

7. National Congress of Neighborhood Women, Statistical sheet on battered women. Undated.

8. *Psychiatric News*. "Incidents of battered wives said under-reported." May 19, 1978, pp. 25-31.

9. Richard J. Gelles, *The Violent Home* (Beverly Hills, Ca: Sage, 1974).

10. See Joseph N. Bell, "Rescuing the Battered Wife" *Human Behavior* (June 1977) pp. 46-50.

11. See Duncan, ibid.

12. Lenore E. Walker, personal communication, December 1978.

13. Sabra F. Wooley, *Battered Women: A Summary* (Washington, DC: WEAL).

14. Irene Hanson Frieze, Research on psychological factors in battered women. Portions from a National Institute of Mental Health grant proposal, November 1, 1976; Gelles, ibid; Langley and Levy, ibid; Del Martin, *Battered Wives* (San Francisco: Glide, 1976).

15. Langley and Levy, ibid.

16. See Frieze, ibid; Gelles, ibid.

17. See George M. Anderson, "Wives, Mothers and Victims" *America*, August 6, 1977, pp. 46-50; Bonnie Carlson, "Battered Women and Their Assailants" *Social Work*, Nov. 1977, pp. 455-460; Fields, ibid; Frieze, ibid; Gelles, ibid; Lisa Leghorn, "Social Responses to Battered Women, Parts 1 and 2" Feminist Alliance Against Rape Newsletter, March/April and May/June 1977, pp. 17-23, 15-19; Martin, ibid; Roy, ibid.

18. Frieze, ibid.

19. Leghorn, ibid.

20. Gelles, ibid.

21. Gelles, ibid.

22. See Business and Professional Women's Foundation, *Info Digest*, Battered Women, March 1977, 12 pp.; Michigan's Women's Commission, ibid.

23. See Jane Roberts Chapman and Margaret Gates (eds.), *The Victimization of Women*, (Beverly Hills, Ca.: Sage, 1978) pp. 111-174; Gelles, ibid; Susan E. Hanks and

C. Peter Rosenbaum "Battered Women: A Study of Women Who Live with Violent Alcohol-Abusing Men" *American Journal of Orthopsychiatry,* 1977, 42:291-306; Martin, ibid.

24. Michigan's Women's Commission, ibid.

25. Erin Pizzey, *Scream Quietly or The Neighbors Will Hear* (Short Hills, NJ: Ridley Enslow, 1977). Lenore E. Walker, *The Battered Woman* (New York: Harper and Row, 1979).

26. Fields, ibid.

27. Diana E. H. Russell and Nicole Van de Ven (eds.) *International Tribunal on Crimes Against Women* (Millbrae, Ca.: Les Femmes, 1976).

28. Bell, ibid.

29. Michigan's Women's Commission, ibid.

30. Langley and Levy, ibid.

31. See Chapman and Gates, ibid; Fields, ibid; *Human Behavior* "Black and Blue Marriages" June 1976, pp. 47-48.

32. Colorado Advisory Committee, U.S. Commission on Civil Rights. *The Silent Victims: Denver's Battered Women,* August 1977.

33. Chapman and Gates, ibid; Duncan, ibid.

34. Chapman and Gates, ibid; Langley and Levy, ibid.

35. *Human Behavior,* ibid.

36. Bell, ibid.

37. Frieze, ibid.

38. Ibid.

39. Gelles, ibid.

40. *Human Behavior.* "The Paralysis of the Battered Wife" May 1977, pp. 47-48.

41. Chapman and Gates, ibid; Karl Schonborn, *To Keep the Peace: Crisis Management in Law Enforcement* (Ca: Law Enforcement Assistance Administration, 1976).

42. Marcia Rockwood, "Courts and Cops." *Ms.,* April 1977, p. 19.

43. James H. Rich, "Family Violence is a New Area of Congressional Concern" *Child Abuse and Neglect Report,* March 1978.

Notes to Chapter 1

1. Del Martin, *Battered Wives* (San Francisco: Glide Publications, 1976) pp. 1-4.

2. Rodney Stark and James McEvoy III, "Middle-Class Violence," *Psychology Today* (November, 1970) pp. 30-31.

3. Karen Durbin, "Wife-Beating," *Ladies Home Journal* (June 1974) p. 64.

4. Northeast Patrol Division Task Force, Kansas City Police Department, "Conflict Management: Analysis/Resolution," 1973.

5. Murray A. Straus, "Normative and Behavioral Aspects of Violence Between Spouses: Preliminary Data on a Nationally Representative U.S.A. Sample," University of New Hampshire, 1977.

6. Lenore Walker, "The Battered Women Syndrome Revisited: Psycho-social Theories." Paper presented at the meeting of the American Psychological Association, San Francisco, 1977.

7. Robert N. Whitehurst, "Violence in Husband-Wife Interaction," in Suzanne Steinmetz and Murray Straus (eds.) *Violence in the Family* (New York: Dodd, Mead, 1975), pp. 78-79.

8. Elaine Hilberman and Kit Munson, "Sixty Battered Women: A Preliminary Report." Paper presented at the meeting of the American Psychiatric Association, Toronto, 1977.

9. Gene Errington, "Family Violence—Is It a Woman's Problem?" Presentation at Symposium on Family Violence, Vancouver, British Columbia, 1977.

10. J. J. Gayford, "Battered Wives," *Medical Science Law* (1975), Vol. 15, No. 4, pp. 243-244.

11. Jean Baker Miller, *Toward a New Psychology of Women* (Boston: Beacon Press, 1976) pp. 6-7.

12. Karen DeCrow, *Sexist Justice* (New York: Random House, 1974) p. 169.

13. I. K. Broverman et al. "Sex Role Stereotypes and Clinical Judgments of Mental Health," *Journal of Consulting and Clinical Psychology,* 1970, 34: 1-7.

14. Ruth Pancoast and Lynda Weston, "Feminist Psychotherapy: A Method for Fighting Social Control of Women," a position statement of the Feminist Counseling Collective, Washington, D.C., 1974.

15. Donald Moreland, "Why Are Men Angry at Women?" Presentation at conference on Battered Women, American Friends Service Committee, New York, 1977 .

16. Frederick Engels, *The Origin of Family, Private Property and the State* (Moscow: Progress, 1948) p. 53.

17. Elizabeth Gould Davis, *The First Sex* (New York: Putnam, 1971) p. 255.

18. Barbara Hirsch, *Divorce: What a Woman Needs to Know* (New York: Bantam, 1973) pp. 9-10.

19. Lenore Weitzman, "Legal Regulation of Marriage: Tradition and Change," *California Law Review,* 1974, Vol. 62, No. 4, p. 1170.

20. W. Blackstone, *Commentaries,* 1765, p. 442.

21. Hernan San Martin, "Machismo: Latin America's Myth-Cult of Male Supremacy," *UNESCO Courier* (March, 1975).

22. Jessie Bernard, *The Future of Marriage* (New York: Bantam, 1973) pp. 3-58.

23. Aaron Rutledge, "The Feudal System of Marriage," *San Francisco Chronicle* (May 26, 1977).

24. Weitzman, p. 1277, n. 483.

25. William Mandel, *Soviet Women* (Garden City, N.Y.: Anchor, 1975) pp. 13-14.

26. Davis, p. 311.

27. Robert Calvert, "Criminal and Civil Liability in Husband-Wife Assaults," in Suzanne Steinmetz and Murray Straus (eds.) *Violence in the Family* (New York: Dodd, Mead, 1975) pp. 88-89.

28. Donald Dutton, "Domestic Dispute Intervention by Police." Presentation at Symposium on Family Violence, Vancouver, British Columbia, 1977.

29. Sue Eisenberg and Patricia Micklow, "The Assaulted Wife: 'Catch 22' Revisited," University of Michigan, 1974.

30. "Techniques of Dispute Intervention," *Training Bulletin III-J,* City of Oakland Police Services (June 19, 1975) pp. 2-3.

31. Morton Bard and Joseph Zacker, *The Police and Interpersonal Conflict* (Washington, D.C.: Police Foundation, 1976) p. 58.

32. Morton Bard, *The Function of the Police in Crisis Intervention and Conflict Management.* (Washington, D.C.: U.S. Department of Justice, Law Enforcement Assistance Administration, 1975) pp. 6.9-6.10.

33. Robert B. Murphy et al. "Training Patrolmen as Crisis Intervention Instructors." Unpublished manuscript.

34. James Bannon, "Law Enforcement Problems with Intra-Family Violence." Paper presented at American Bar Association Annual Conference, Montreal, 1975.

35. Adolph W. Hart, "Thomas Promised That He Would," *The New York Times* (June 10, 1975).

36. Trude Fisher, with Marion P. Winston, "The Grim Plight of Destitute Mothers Who Need Free Rooms on a Stormy Night," *Los Angeles Times* (March 12, 1973) Part II, p. 7.

37. J. J. Gayford, "Wife Battering: A Preliminary Survey of 100 Cases," *British Medical Journal* (January 25, 1975) pp. 194-197.

38. Based on data from Eckhardt, "Deviance Visibility and Legal Action: The Duty to Support," *Social Problems,* Vol. 15 (1968) pp. 470, 473-474.

39. James W. Prescott, "Body Pleasure and the Origins of Violence," *Bulletin of the Atomic Sciences* (November, 1975) pp. 10-20.

40. Lawrence Van Gelder, "Giving Battered Wives a Little Legal Clout," *The New York Times* (November 13, 1976).

41. "Needs of Battered Women Receive Special Attention From Milwaukee D.A.'s Office," *Response* (February 1977) Vol. 1, No. 3, pp. 1-2.

42. Report from the Select Committee on Violence in Marriage. (London: Her Majesty's Stationery Office, 1975) p. IX.

Notes to Chapter 2

1. Murray Straus et al. Violence in the family: An assessment of knowledge and research needs. Paper given before the American Association for the Advancement of Science. Boston, 1976.

2. D. Besherov, Testimony to Congress on child abuse and neglect. Congressional Committee on Science and Technology. February 1978.

3. L. E. Walker, *The Battered Woman* (New York: Harper & Row, 1979).

Note to Chapter 4

1. See 22 documented cases collected in footnote 3, page 143, of Schneider and Jordan, "Representation of Women Who Defend Themselves in Response to Physical or Sexual Assault," *Women's Rights Law Reporter,* Spring 1978, Vol. 4, No. 3.

Notes to Appendix A

1. A felony is a serious crime punishable by imprisonment in a state prison; a misdemeanor is less serious and is punishable by a fine or county jail term of less than one year.

2. Crimes are divided into two classifications: felony and misdemeanor. A felony is a more serious crime than a misdemeanor and carries a heavier punishment. Battery and assault with a deadly weapon are felonies when the injuries are serious. Wife beating is always a felony.

ABOUT THE AUTHORS

SANDRA BLAIR, M. A. and J. D., is an attorney in private practice in San Francisco. Ms. Blair has an adjunct faculty appointment at Hastings College of Law and is actively involved in legal organizations working on issues affecting women and their families. She has lectured widely on both women and law and family law.

DEL MARTIN, a consultant, writer, and lecturer, is Coordinator of the National Organization for Women's National Task Force on Battered Women/Household Violence. She is a commissioner and past chairperson of the San Francisco Commission on the Status of Women and is active on the commission's Violent Crimes Against Women Committee. Ms. Martin is the author of *Battered Wives* (1976), the first book-length study of battering in this country, and a work which has led both to her being recognized as the foremost expert on battered women and to the increased interest on the part of many others in curbing domestic violence. Since the publication of *Battered Wives,* public and private funding has become available for research, public education, and shelters. Ms. Martin has published widely on the topic in newspapers, magazines, and professional journals; she has also lectured at both professional and nonprofessional conferences on battering and other feminist issues.

DONNA M. MOORE, M. A., is currently completing her Ph.D. in social-personality psychology from the University of California, Davis, while also working as the Human Resources and Affirmative Action Officer at Montana State University. She was previously Program Director of the Women's Resources and Research Center, University of California, Davis and chaired the planning committee for the Battered Women's Conference which led to publication of this book. Ms. Moore has long been active in feminist and human rights issues. She was co-founder of the Yolo County Sexual Assault Center and the Davis Battered Women's Network while living in northern California and has lectured widely on topics regarding psychology and women.

EVA JEFFERSON PATERSON, J. D., is Assistant Director of the San Francisco Lawyers' Committee for Urban Affairs where she designs and implements law reform litigation and projects, and administers a free legal aid clinic staffed by attorneys from some of the major San Francisco law firms who provide their services on a free basis as part of their commitment to *pro bono* legal aid. Ms. Paterson completed her B.A. in Political Science in 1971 from Northwestern University where she began a long history of actively working toward improving community, political, and legal circumstances for the poor, minority groups, and women. Since being admitted to the California Bar in 1975 after graduation from law school at the University of California, Berkeley, she has worked on litigation affecting both minorities and women. Ms. Paterson has been one of the most actively involved attorneys in *Scott v. Hart,* a class action suit brought by and on behalf of battered women in Oakland who charged that they have received little or no physical protection from the Oakland Police Department. That case recently resulted in the Oakland Police Department agreeing to change its policies regarding domestic violence in an effort to help battered women.

FRAN PEPITONE-ROCKWELL, Ph.D., is a clinical psychologist with an appointment as Assistant Professor in the School of Medicine, Department of Psychiatry, and is also the Academic Director of the Women's Resources and Research Center, University of California, Davis. Dr. Pepitone-Rockwell spent the 1960s working as a psychiatric nurse in a number of settings. In 1972 she returned to school at the California School of Professional Psychology in San Francisco where she received her Ph.D. in Clinical Psychology in 1974. Since receiving her Ph.D. she has been actively involved in activities which combine her clinical training and her feminist interests. She has served widely as a consultant and participant in community projects working with suicide, rape, families and children, and battered women. Dr. Pepitone-Rockwell conducts couples therapy with her husband, Don Rockwell, M.D., and lectures, researches, and writes on issues which affect the attitudes about and treatment of women by professionals who serve them.

LENORE E. WALKER is a licensed psychologist and Chairperson and Associate Professor of Psychology at Colorado Women's College in Denver where she also conducts a private clinical practice. Dr. Walker received her master's degree from the City University of New

York in 1967 and her Ed.D. from Rutgers University in 1972; she also received graduate clinical training at both Rutgers University and Harvard Medical School. She was on the faculty at Rutgers Medical School prior to moving to Denver in 1975. Dr. Walker has worked as a clinical and school psychologist for the past 12 years during which she has developed and maintained an active interest in feminist issues and their relationship to the practice of psychotherapy. Her interest in both feminist issues and battered women is demonstrated by extensive articles, book chapters, and lectures to both professional and nonprofessional audiences. Dr. Walker is currently conducting a large-scale research project funded by the National Institute of Mental Health on battered women and has a book on interviews with battered women published by Harper and Row in January 1979.